Quick
Knitted
Afghans™

Edited by Jeanne Stauffer

Exclusively using Plymouth yarns

HOUSE of
WHITE
BIRCHES
PUBLISHERS
SINCE 1947

Quick Knitted Afghans

Editor: Jeanne Stauffer
Associate Editors: Dianne Schmidt, Barb Sprunger
Book and Cover Design: Jessi Butler
Pattern Editor: E. Joy Slayton
Design Manager: Vicki Blizzard
Copy Editors: Nicki Lehman, Mary Martin, Alice Rice
Publications Coordinator: Tanya Turner

Photography: Jeff Chilcote, Tammy Christian, Kelly Heydinger, Justin P. Wiard
Photography Assistant: Linda Quinlan

Production Coordinator and Artist: Brenda Gallmeyer
Production Assistant: Janet Bowers, Marj Morgan
Traffic Coordinator: Sandra Beres
Technical Artists: Leslie Brandt, Julie Catey, Chad Summers

Publishers: Carl H. Muselman, Arthur K. Muselman
Chief Executive Officer: John Robinson
Marketing Director: Scott Moss
Book Marketing Manager: Craig Scott
Product Development Director: Vivian Rothe
Publishing Services Manager: Brenda R. Wendling

Printed in the United States of America
First Printing: 2001
Library of Congress Number: 00-112318
ISBN: 1-882138-80-5

Welcome!

We had a great time planning this book for you. We started by talking to the good people at Plymouth Yarn Co. about their wonderful yarns!

Their dedication in offering unsurpassed quality in hand-knitting yarns which are available in over 1,000 retail stores (check www.plymouthyarn.com for locating a store near you), and the wide variety of yarns they offer made them the perfect source of yarn for this book. Plymouth Yarn Company, Inc., located in Bristol, Pa., is a spin-off of a fiber company started in 1964 by Richard Power, Sr. and partners. Ownership remains in the Power family and their dedication to quality in hand knitting remains constant.

Of course, for a book of afghan patterns, we first looked at Plymouth Encore, a wool acrylic blend that is machine washable and machine dryable, perfect for afghans! It comes in three weights: worsted, DK and chunky.

Plymouth's oldest hand-knitting yarn, Galway, is also a popular yarn for afghans. This worsted weight, 100 percent virgin wool yarn also comes in a wide variety of colors, especially when you add Galway Highland Heathers and Galway Colornep.

For our summer throws, we selected Wildflower (51 percent mercerized cotton, 49 percent acrylic), a DK weight yarn perfect for lighter, more delicate throws. It comes in lovely pastels and floral shades.

Whether you knit these afghans as gifts for family or friends, to enter the county fair, to give to charitable causes, or to snuggle up in with one of your children, I know you'll find them a pleasure to knit and share.

Warmest regards,

Jeanne Stauffer

Contents

Summer Days

*A*s the sun sets after a warm sunshiny day, you'll enjoy wrapping up in one of these breezy and beautiful afghans. With their open patterns and summery colors, they're just right for keeping out the cool air while adding a colorful touch to your home.

Chapter 1

Lazy Man's Plaid

Design by Barbara Venishnick

Brightly colored rows with a slip stitch background combine with a mitered border and tassels to create this handsome afghan.

Skill Level
Intermediate***

Finished Size
Approximately 44 x 56 inches

Materials
- Plymouth Wildflower DK weight 51 percent mercerized cotton/49 percent acrylic yarn (137 yds/50g per ball): 12 balls purple #45 (A), 4 balls each orange #56 (B), green #58 (C), yellow #48 (D)
- Size 11 (8mm) 29-inch circular needle or size needed to obtain gauge
- Size H/8 (5mm) crochet hook for cast on
- Tapestry needle

Gauge
12½ sts and 22 rows = 4 inches/10cm in pat with 2 strands held tog

To save time, take time to check gauge.

Pattern Notes
Afghan is worked with 2 strands of yarn held tog throughout.

When working pat, sl sts purlwise with yarn on WS of fabric.

Work first and last sts of every row in selvage st: k first st tbl, sl last st wyib. Selvage sts are not included in pat instructions.

Special Abbreviation
M1 (Make 1): Inc by making a back-

ward loop over right needle.

Special Technique
Provisional cast on: With crochet hook and scrap yarn, ch number of sts needed for cast on plus a few extra. With working yarn and needle, pick up 1 st in back purl bump of each ch st until desired number of sts is cast on.

Afghan
With A, provisionally cast on 129 sts (127 for pat + 1 selvage st on each side).

Note: Cast on row is counted as Row 1 of pat for first rep.

Row 1 (RS): With A, knit.

Row 2: With A, purl.

Rows 3–6: With B, [k3, sl 1] 31 times, end k3.

Row 7: With A, knit.

Row 8: With A, purl.

Rows 9 and 10: With C, k1, [sl 1, k3] 31 times, end sl 1, k1.

Row 11: With A, knit.

Row 12: With A, purl.

Rows 13–16: With D, [k3, sl 1] 31 times, end k3.

Row 17: With A, knit.

Row 18: With A, purl.

Rows 19 and 20: With C, k1, [sl 1, k3] 31 times, end sl 1, k1.

[Rep Rows 1–20] 12 more times. [Rep Rows 1–8] once more.

Top Border
Row 1: With A, knit all sts across (including selvage sts).

Row 2: With A, knit across.

Row 3: With C, k1, M1, k127, M1, k1.

Row 4: With C, k131.

Row 5: With A, k1, M1, k129, M1, k1.

Row 6: With A, k133.

Row 7: With D, k1, M1, k131, M1, k1.

Row 8: With D, k135.

Row 9: With A, k1, M1, k133, M1, k1.

Row 10: With A, k137.

Row 11: With B, k1, M1, k135, M1, k1.

Row 12: With B, k139.

Row 13: With A, k1, M1, k137, M1, k1.

Bind off all sts knitwise on WS.

Bottom Border
Undo crochet ch and place sts on needle. Work as for top border.

Side Border
Row 1: With A and circular needle, RS facing, pick up and k 1 st in first row of bottom border, 1 st in every selvage st along side, and 1 st in first row of top border, turn.

Row 2: With A, knit back, turn.

Row 3: With C, pick up and k 1 st in color C row of bottom border, knit across all sts of previous row, pick up and k 1 st in color C row of top border, turn.

Row 4: With C, knit back, turn.

Continue in this fashion, picking up 1 more st at beg and end of each RS row, using same color sequence as for top and bottom borders.

Bind off on last WS row with A as for top and bottom borders.

Tassels
Make 4

Wrap a double strand of A around a 6-inch ruler or cardboard 35 times. Tie at top and cut bottom ends. With A, wrap tightly 1 inch below top tie. Using 1 strand each of B, C and D, wrap once around 1 inch below top tie, covering color A wrap. Tie strands tightly and using a tapestry needle, run ends into center of tassel. Trim bottom of tassel ends evenly. Attach 1 tassel to each corner of afghan. ◆

Guy's Guernsey Afghan

Design by Lois S. Young

The stitch pattern on this afghan was inspired by patterns on English Guernsey sweaters worn by fishermen.

Skill Level
Easy**

Finished Size
Approximately 48 x 64 inches

Materials
- Plymouth Fantasy Naturale worsted weight 100 percent cotton yarn (140 yds/100g per ball): 15 balls taupe #7360
- Size 9 (5.5mm) 29-inch circular needle or size needed to obtain gauge
- Cable needle
- Tapestry needle

Gauge
16 sts and 24 rows = 4 inches/10cm in St st

To save time, take time to check gauge.

Pattern Note
Sl first st of each row knitwise.

Special Abbreviation
M1 (Make 1): Inc by making a backward loop over right needle.

Pattern Stitch
(multiple of 24 sts + 22)

Rows 1, 3, 7 and 9 (RS): Sl 1, k6, *p1, k6, p1, k16, rep from *, end last rep k7 instead of k16.

Rows 2, 4, 6 and 8: Sl 1, k4, p2, *k1, p6, k1, p16, rep from *, end last rep p2, k5 instead of p16.

Row 5: Sl 1, k6, p1, *sl next 3 sts to cn, hold in front, k3, return sts from cn to left needle and k3, p18, rep from *end last rep p1, k7 instead of p18.

Row 10: Rep Row 2.

Rep Rows 1–10 for pat.

Afghan
Loosely cast on 182 sts.

Border
Rows 1–7: Sl 1, knit across.

Set up pat: Sl 1, k6, *p1, k3, M1, k2, p1, k16, rep from *, end last rep k7 instead of k16. (190 sts)

Work Rows 2–10 of pat, then work [Rows 1–10] 35 times. Rep [Rows 1–8] once more.

Dec row: Sl 1, k6, *p1, k3, k2tog, k1, p1, k16, rep from *, end last rep k7 instead of k16. (182 sts)

Border
Rows 1–6: Sl 1, knit across. Bind off knitwise on WS.

Block lightly. ◆

Lacy Twist Afghan

Design by Lois S. Young

The stitch pattern of this afghan was inspired by patterns from German folk stockings.

Skill Level
Intermediate***

Finished Measurements
Approximately 52 inches by 54 inches, excluding fringe

Materials
- Plymouth Fantasy Naturale worsted weight 100 percent cotton yarn (140 yds/100g per ball): 14 balls olive green #5606
- Size 9 (5.5mm) 29-inch circular needle or size needed to obtain gauge
- Cable needle
- Tapestry needle
- Size H/8 (5mm) crochet hook for fringe

Gauge
14 sts (1 pat rep) and 20 rows (2½ pat reps) = 4 inches/10cm

To save time, take time to check gauge.

Pattern Note
Sl first st of each row as if to knit.

Pattern Stitch
(multiple of 14 sts + 10)

Rows 1, 5 and 7 (RS): Sl 1, k1, p1, *k1, yo, p2tog, k1, p3, k2, yo, ssk, p3, rep from * to last 7 sts, k1, yo, p2tog, k1, p1, k2.

Rows 2, 4, 6 and 8: Sl 1, k2, *p1, yo, p2tog, p1, k3, p2, yo, p2tog, k3, rep from * to last 7 sts, p1, yo, p2tog, p1, k3.

Row 3: Sl 1, k1, p1, *k1, yo, p2tog, k1, p3, sl next 2 sts to cn and hold in back, k2, replace sts from cn on LH needle, yo, ssk (cable cross worked), p3, rep from * to last 7 sts, k1, yo, p2tog, k1, p1, k2.

Row 8: Rep Row 2.

Rep Rows 1–8 for pat.

Afghan
Cast on 206 sts.

Next row (WS): Sl 1, k to end of row.

[Work pat Rows 1–8] 32 times. [Rep Rows 1–5] once.

Bind off knitwise on WS. Block lightly.

Fringe
For each fringe, cut 4 (11½-inch) lengths of yarn. Beg at 1 corner of top or bottom of afghan, with WS facing, *fold strands in half. Insert crochet hook from WS to RS of fabric in center edge st of openwork panel or lace cable. Pull strands through to make a loop, pull ends through loop and tighten up. Rep from * in each openwork panel and lace cable. ◆

Little Buds Afghan

Design by Laura Polley

Knit this easy lattice pattern with a double strand of yarn for quick results.

Skill Level
Intermediate***

Finished Size
Approximately 56 x 61 inches (lightly blocked)

Materials
- Plymouth Wildflower DK weight 51 percent mercerized cotton/49 percent acrylic yarn (137 yds/50g per ball): 30 balls off-white #40
- Size 11 (8mm) 32-inch circular needle or size needed to obtain gauge
- Stitch markers
- Tapestry needle

Gauge
11 sts = 4 inches/10cm in garter st with 2 strands of yarn held tog

To save time, take time to check gauge.

Pattern Notes
Afghan is worked with 2 strands of yarn held tog throughout.

Circular needle is used to accomodate large number of sts. Do not join at end of row.

Special Abbreviation
Sk2p: Sl next st knitwise, k2tog, pass sl st over k2tog.

Pattern Stitch
(multiple of 6 sts + 1)

Row 1 (RS): K1, *yo, p1, p3tog, p1, yo, k1, rep from * across.

Rows 2, 4 and 6: Purl.

Row 3: K2, yo, sk2p, yo, *k3, yo, sk2p, yo, rep from * to last 2 sts, end k2.

Row 5: P2tog, p1, yo, k1, yo, p1, *p3tog, p1, yo, k1, yo, p1, rep from * to last 2 sts, end p2tog.

Row 7: K2tog, yo, k3, yo, *sk2p, yo, k3, yo, rep from * to last 2 sts, end ssk.

Row 8: Purl.

Rep Rows 1–8 for pat.

Afghan
With 2 strands of yarn held tog, cast on 165 sts. Knit 8 rows.

Beg pat
Row 1: K4, pm, work Row 1 of pat over center 157 sts, pm, end k4.

Row 2: K4, work Row 2 of pat over center 157 sts, k4.

Continue in pat as established, keeping first and last 4 sts in garter st throughout, until Rows 1–8 of pat have been worked 33 times, then work [Rows 1–7] once more.

Next row (WS): Knit.

Knit 6 more rows. Bind off all sts loosely.

Finishing
Block. ◆

Dover Road

Design by Elizabeth Mattfield

Garter stitch squares with the ridges running in alternate directions plus garter stitch squares knit from corner to corner provide the texture in this afghan.

Skill Level

Beginner*

Finished Size

Approximately 50 x 60 inches

Materials

- Plymouth Wildflower DK weight 51 percent mercerized cotton/49 percent acrylic yarn (137 yds/50g per ball): 1 ball each apricot #13, beige #16, pale green #19, light sage green #20, gray #30, khaki #31, rose #32, light denim #33, denim #34, sage green #35, cream #40, white #41, soft green #42, turquoise #43, purple #45, black #47, yellow #48, green #49, lilac #50, soft yellow #51, peach #52, pale pink #53, pink #54, bright turquoise #55, orange #56, lime #58, bright pink #59, navy #60, brown #69, pale blue #70
- Size 10½ (6.5mm) needles or size needed to obtain gauge
- Tapestry needle

Gauge

14 sts = 4 inches/10cm in garter st with 2 strands of yarn held tog

To save time, take time to check gauge.

Pattern Notes

Blocks are knitted individually with doubled yarn. Each block will use almost exactly a full ball of yarn, so

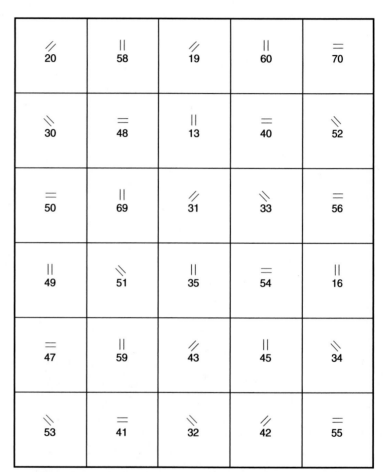

Note: Numbers indicate color; lines represent direction of garter ridges.

FIG. 1

work first block as a swatch. If you are running out of yarn before block is square, start over with 1 or 2 fewer sts. Diagonal blocks will also need to be correspondingly smaller; reduce longest row by approximately same number of sts.

Gauge is somewhat looser than usual for better drape, so relationship between rows and sts may not be quite square. Block might be square several rows sooner than expected.

Diagonal blocks are optional. If preferred, all blocks may be knitted straight, then sewn together like a checkerboard, alternating horizontal and vertical ridges. Sample afghan is made from 18 square blocks and 12 diagonal blocks.

Square Blocks

(sample used colors #13, 16, 35, 40, 41, 45, 47, 48, 49, 50, 54, 55, 56, 58, 59, 60, 67, 69, 70)

Leaving a 24-inch tail for sewing up, cast on 34 sts and work in garter st until block is square (approximately 32 rows). Bind off all sts, leaving a 24-inch tail.

Diagonal Blocks

(sample used colors #19, 20, 30, 31, 32, 33, 34, 42, 43, 51, 52, 53)

Leaving a 24-inch tail for sewing up, cast on 2 sts. Knit 1 row.

Working in garter st, k in front and back of first st every row until there are 43 sts on needle.

Beg on next row, k2tog at beg of every row until 2 sts remaining. Bind off remaining sts, leaving a 24-inch tail.

Finishing

Referring to Fig. 1, sew blocks tog. ◆

Ebb Tide

Design by Barbara Venishnick

This solid-colored afghan combines reverse stockinette stitch, a large cable and lace to produce an afghan rich in texture.

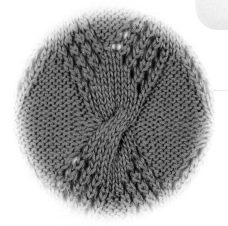

Skill Level
Intermediate***

Finished Size
Approximately 40 x 48 inches

Materials
- Plymouth Fantasy Naturale worsted weight 100 percent cotton yarn (140 yds/100g per ball): 10 balls green #5382
- Size 10 (6mm) 29-inch circular needle or size needed to obtain gauge
- Cable needle
- Size H/8 (5mm) crochet hook
- Tapestry needle

Gauge
16 sts and 22 rows = 4 inches/ 10cm in pat

To save time, take time to check gauge.

Pattern Note
Circular needle is used to accomodate large number of sts. Do not join at end of row.

Special Abbreviations
S (Selvage st): At beg of every row, k1 tbl; at end of every row, sl 1 purlwise wyif.

C9F (Cable 9): Sl 5 sts to cn, hold in back, k4, sl last st on cn back to LH needle, k1, k4 from cn.

K1b: Knit stitch in back loop.

Afghan
Cast on 165 sts.

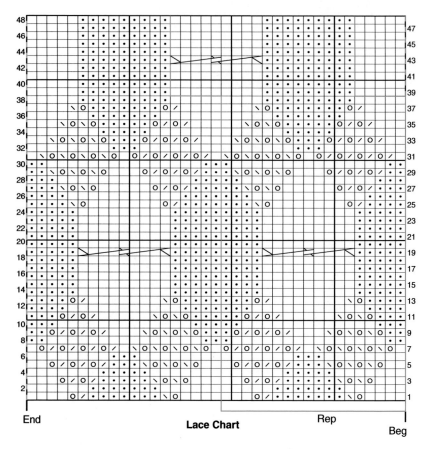

Lace Chart

End · · · Rep · · · Beg

Row 1 (RS): S, [k4, yo, ssk, p7, k2tog, yo, k3] 8 times, k4, yo, ssk, p7, k2tog, yo, p4, S.

Rows 2, 4 and 6: S, p the yo and knit sts, k the purl sts of previous row, S.

Row 3: S, [k3, {yo, ssk} twice, p5, {k2tog, yo} twice, k2] 8 times, k3, [yo, ssk] twice, p5, [k2tog, yo] twice, k3, S.

Row 5: S, [k2, {yo, ssk} 3 times, p3, {k2tog, yo} 3 times, k1] 8 times, k2, [yo, ssk] 3 times, p3, [k2tog, yo] 3 times, k2, S.

Row 7: S, [k1, {yo, ssk} 4 times, k1, {k2tog, yo} 4 times] 8 times, k1, [yo, ssk] 4 times, k1, [k2tog, yo] 4 times, k1, S.

Row 8: S, [k2, p15, k1] 8 times, k2,

STITCH KEY
- ☐ K on RS, p on WS
- · P on RS, k on WS
- ☑ K2tog
- ☒ Ssk
- ○ Yo
- C9F

p15, k2, S.

Row 9: S, [p2, {yo, ssk} 3 times, k3, {k2tog, yo} 3 times, p1] 8 times, p2, [yo, ssk] 3 times, k3, [k2tog, yo] 3 times, p2, S.

Row 10: S, [k3, p13, k2] 8 times, k3, p13, k3, S.

Row 11: S, [p3, {yo, ssk} twice, k5, {k2tog, yo} twice, p2] 8 times, p3, [yo,

Row 27: S, [p3, {k2tog, yo} twice, k5, [yo, ssk] twice, p2] 8 times, p3, {k2tog, yo} twice, k5, [yo, ssk] twice, p3, S.

Row 29: S, [p2, {k2tog, yo} 3 times, k3, {yo, ssk} 3 times, p1] 8 times, p2, [k2tog, yo] 3 times, k3, [yo, ssk] 3 times, p2, S.

Row 31: S, [k1, {k2tog, yo} 4 times, k1, {yo, ssk} 4 times] 8 times, k1, [k2tog, yo] 4 times, k1, [yo, ssk] 4 times, k1, S.

Row 32: S, [p8, k3, p7] 8 times, p8, k3, p8, S.

Row 33: S, [k2, {k2tog, yo} 3 times, p3, {yo, ssk} 3 times, k1] 8 times, k2, [k2tog, yo] 3 times, p3, [yo, ssk] 3 times, k2, S.

Row 34: S, [p7, k5, p6] 8 times, p7, k5, p7, S.

Row 35: S, [k3, {k2tog, yo} twice, p5, {yo, ssk} twice, k2] 8 times, k3, [k2tog, yo] twice, p5, [yo, ssk] twice, k3, S.

Row 36: S, [p6, k7, p5] 8 times, p6, k7, p6, S.

Row 37: S, [k4, k2tog, yo, p7, yo, ssk, k3] 8 times, k4, k2tog, yo, p7, yo, ssk, k4, S.

Rows 38, 40 and 42: S, p5, [k9, p9] 8 times, k9, p5, S.

Rows 39 and 41: S, k5, [p9, k9] 8 times, p9, k5, S.

Row 43: S, k5, [p9, C9F] 8 times, p9, k5, S.

Rows 44, 46 and 48: Rep Row 38.

Rows 45 and 47: Rep Row 39.

[Work Rows 1–48] 3 more times, then [rep Rows 1–38] once more. Bind off all sts loosely.

Edging

Cast on 8 sts.

Row 1: K1b, [k2tog, yo] 3 times, k1.

Row 2: P7, sl 1 wyib.

Row 3: K1b, k1, [k2tog, yo] twice, k2.

Row 4: P7, sl 1 wyib.

Rep Rows 1–4 until edging is long enough to go completely around afghan with a bit extra for ease at corners (approximately 170 inches/4¾ yds).

Bind off all sts on RS. Leave ball of yarn attached.

Pin, then sew sl st edge of edging to afghan. Sew bind off and cast on ends tog.

***Note:** Place seam near, but not right at a corner.*

With attached ball and crochet hook, work 3 sc in each large yo space created by Row 1 yarn overs around afghan. ◆

ssk] twice, k5, [k2tog, yo] twice, p3, S.

Row 12: S, [k4, p11, k3] 8 times, k4, p11, k4, S.

Row 13: S, [p4, yo, ssk, k7, k2tog, yo, p3] 8 times, p4, yo, ssk, k7, k2tog, yo, p4, S.

Rows 14, 16 and 18: S, [k5, p9, k4] 8 times, k5, p9, k5, S.

Rows 15 and 17: S, [p5, k9, p4] 8

times, p5, k9, p5, S.

Row 19: S, [p5, C9F, p4] 8 times, p5, C9F, p5, S.

Rows 20, 22 and 24: Rep Row 14.

Rows 21 and 23: Rep Row 15.

Row 25: S, [p4, k2tog, yo, k7, yo, ssk, p3] 8 times, p4, k2tog, yo, k7, yo, ssk, p4, S.

Rows 26, 28 and 30: Rep Row 2.

By the Sea

Design by Kathleen Power Johnson

Combine a lacy shell and wave pattern with seaside colors to create a truly unique summer afghan.

Skill Level

Intermediate***

Finished Size

Approximately 48 x 60 inches

Materials

- Plymouth Fantasy Naturale worsted weight 100 percent cotton yarn (140 yds/100g per ball): 11 balls variegated #9936
- Size 10 (6mm) needles or size needed to obtain gauge
- Crochet hook (for fringe)

Gauge

14 sts and 24 rows = 4 inches/ 10cm in garter st

To save time, take time to check gauge.

Pattern Note

Double-Wrapped Sts: When knitting or slipping these sts on following row, drop 2nd wrap.

Pattern Stitch

Shell and Wave Pat

(multiple of 12 sts + 1)

Row 1: Knit across, wrapping yarn twice around needle for each st.

Row 2: Sl 4 sts purlwise, insert LH needle into front of these 4 sts from left to right and k4tog, *yo, [k1, yo] 5 times, sl 7 sts purlwise, insert LH needle into front of these 7 sts from left to right and k7tog, rep from *, ending last rep sl 4, insert LH needle into front of these 4 sts from left to right and k4tog.

Row 3: Knit across (there should be one yo after each st except last st).

Rows 4, 5 and 6: Knit.

Rep Rows 1–6 for pat.

Afghan

Cast on 169 sts. Knit 6 rows, then beg pat. Work even in pat until afghan measures approximately 59½ inches, ending with Row 6. K 3 rows. Bind off all sts.

Fringe

For each end, cut 96 (15-inch) strands. Beg at corner, *fold 3 strands in half, pull through st and knot close to afghan edge. Rep from * every 1½ inches across. ◆

Garden Delights

*B*eautiful Afghans with floral designs three-dimensional flowers and textured designs reminiscent of nature combine to create this bouquet of afghans ready to warm you on a cool spring evening. Knit a spring beauty to warm your heart and your soul.

Chapter 2

Blossoms & Buds

Design by Diane Zangl

Knitting, crochet, and embroidery combine on this flower-strewn, crib-size afghan. It is sure to become a treasured heirloom.

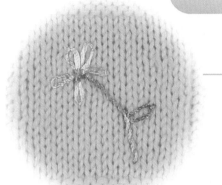

Skill Level
Easy**

Finished Measurements
Approximately 42 x 56 inches

Materials
- Plymouth Galway worsted weight 100 percent wool yarn (230 yds/200g per ball): 8 balls natural #0l
- Rayon embroidery floss from DMC (8.7 yds per skein): 7 skeins green #30503, 3 skeins each peach #30352, yellow #30744, and blue #33325
- Size 5 (3.75mm) 24-inch circular needle or size needed to obtain gauge
- Size F/5 (3.75mm) crochet hook
- Fray Check

Gauge
18 sts and 24 rows = 4 inches/10cm in St st

To save time, take time to check gauge.

Pattern Stitch
Squares Pat (multiple of 30 sts + 15)

Row 1(RS): K15, *p15, k15, rep from * across.

Row 2: P15, *k15, p15, rep from * across.

Rows 3–20: Rep Rows 1 and 2.

Row 21: Rep Row 2.

Row 22: Rep Row 1.

Rows 23–40: Rep Rows 21 and 22.

Rep Rows 1–40 for pat.

Afghan
Cast on 195 sts.

[Work pat Rows 1–40] 7 times. [Rep Rows 1–20] once.

Bind off all sts, do not cut yarn.

Edging
Row 1: Using last bind off lp as first crochet st, work 1 row sc around entire afghan, making sure to keep work flat. Sl st to join.

Row 2: *Ch 6, sk 2 sc, sl st in next sc, rep from * around. Sl st to top of first ch-6 lp.

Row 3: *Ch 6, sl st in center of ch-6 sp, rep from * around. Sl st to join. Cut yarn.

Embroidery
Flowers are worked on St st (knit) squares only. Work Fig. 1 flowers on rows with 7 knit squares and Fig. 2 flowers on rows with 6 knit squares.

Referring to photo, work in color sequence of peach, yellow, then blue. All stems and leaves are green.

To prevent embroidery from slipping, apply a small dot of Fray Check to each end of thread immediately on completion of flower. ◆

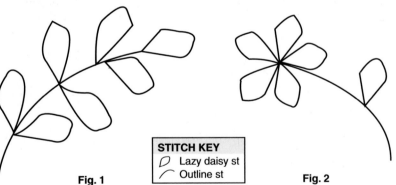

STITCH KEY
⬭ Lazy daisy st
⌒ Outline st

Fig. 1

Fig. 2

Summer Garden Coverlet

Design by Kathleen Power Johnson

Quick-to-knit panels combine to turn a solid color into a multi-textured coverlet.

Skill Level
Intermediate***

Finished Size
Approximately 48 x 60 inches

Materials
- Plymouth Wildflower DK weight 51 percent mercerized cotton/49 percent acrylic yarn (137 yds/50g per ball): 32 balls green #11
- Size 9 (5.5mm) needles or size needed to obtain gauge
- Size 10½ (6.5mm) needles
- Tapestry needle

Gauge
17 sts and 23 rows = 4 inches/10cm in pat with smaller needles and 2 strands of yarn

To save time, take time to check gauge.

Pattern Note
Afghan is worked with 2 strands of yarn held tog throughout.

Special Abbreviation
Twist 3: K3tog but do not sl off needle. K first st on LH needle and sl off needle, knit 2nd st in same way, sl last st off needle without knitting it.

Pattern Stitches
Cable & Leaf Panel (33 sts)

Row 1 (RS): P2, *k7, p3, k3, p3, rep from *, end last rep p2.

Row 2 and all even rows: Purl.

Row 3: P2, *k7, p3, twist 3, p3, rep from *, end last rep p2.

Row 5: P2, *ssk, k3, k2tog, p3, [k1, yo] twice, k1, p3, rep from *, end last rep p2.

Row 7: P2, *ssk, k1, k2tog, p3, k2, yo, k1, yo, k2, p3, rep from *, end p2.

Row 9: P2, *twist 3, p3, k7, p3, rep from *, end p2.

Row 11: P2, *k3, p3, k7, p3, rep from *, end p2.

Row 13: Rep Row 9.

Row 15: P2, *[k1, yo] twice, k1, p3, ssk, k3, k2tog, p3, rep from *, end p2.

Row 17: P2, *k2, yo, k1, yo, k2, p3, ssk, k1, k2tog, p3, rep from *, end p2.

Row 19: Rep Row 3.

Row 20: Purl.

Rep Rows 1–20 for pat.

Fencepost Lace Panel (49 sts)

Rows 1 and 3 (WS): K1, p1, *k3, p1, rep from *, end k3.

Rows 2 and 6: Knit.

Row 4: K1, k2tog, *yo, k1, yo, k3tog, rep from *, end yo, k2.

Rows 5 and 7: K3, *p1, k3, rep from *, end p1, k1.

Row 8: K2, yo, *k3tog, yo, k1, yo, rep from *, end k2tog, k1.

Rep Rows 1–8 for pat.

Cable & Leaf Panel
Make 3

With smaller needles and 2 strands of yarn, cast on 33 sts and work in pat for 330 rows, ending with Row 10 (approximately 58 inches), maintaining purl garter selvage throughout. Bind off all sts.

Fencepost Panel
Make 2

With smaller needles and 2 strands of yarn, cast on 49 sts and work in pat for 330 rows, ending with Row 2 (approximately 58 inches), maintaining knit garter selvage throughout. Bind off all sts.

Finishing
Assemble panels in this sequence: leaf—lace—leaf—lace—leaf. Sew with a single strand of yarn, working from a garter st bump on 1 edge to a corresponding bump on opposite edge for a nearly invisible seam.

Border
On lower edge with RS facing and smaller needles, pick up and k 212 sts, knit 6 rows. Bind off with larger needles.

Rep for top edge. Damp block if necessary. ◆

Counterpane Afghan

Design by Nazanin S. Fard

A lovely leaf pattern design creates this beautiful afghan. Each piece is worked in a triangle, then combined to form squares of leaves.

Skill Level

Intermediate***

Finished Size

Approximately 64 x 43 inches

Materials

- Plymouth Wildflower DK weight 51 percent mercerized cotton/49 percent acrylic yarn (137 yds/50g per ball): 30 balls peach #13
- Size 8 (5mm) needles or size needed to obtain gauge
- Size F/5 (3.75mm) crochet hook
- Tapestry needle

Gauge

16 sts and 24 rows = 4 inches/ 10cm with 2 strands of yarn held tog

To save time, take time to check gauge.

Pattern Note

Afghan is worked with 2 strands of yarn held tog throughout.

Triangle

Make 96

With 2 strands of yarn, cast on 5 sts.

Row 1 (RS): P5.

Row 2: K1, yo, k1, p1, k1, yo, k1. (7 sts)

Row 3: P3, k1, p3.

Row 4: K1, yo, k2, p1, k2, yo, k1. (9 sts)

Row 5: P4, k1, p4.

Row 6: K1, yo, k3, p1, k3, yo, k1. (11 sts)

Row 7: P3, p2tog, yo, k1, yo, p2tog, p3.

Row 8: K1, yo, k3, p3, k3, yo, k1. (13 sts)

Row 9: P3, p2tog, [k1, yo] twice, k1, p2tog, p3.

Row 10: K1, yo, k3, p5, k3, yo, k1. (15 sts)

Row 11: P3, p2tog, k2, yo, k1, yo, k2, p2tog, p3.

Row 12: K1, yo, k3, p7, k3, yo, k1. (17 sts)

Row 13: P3, p2tog, k3, yo, k1, yo, k3, p2tog, p3.

Row 14: K1, yo, k3, p9, k3, yo, k1. (19 sts)

Row 15: P5, yo, ssk, k5, k2tog, yo, p5.

Row 16: K1, yo, k5, p7, k5, yo, k1. (21 sts)

Row 17: P7, yo, ssk, k3, k2tog, yo, p7.

Row 18: K1, yo, k7, p5, k7, yo, k1. (23 sts)

Row 19: P9, yo, ssk, k1, k2tog, yo, p9.

Row 20: K1, yo, k9, p3, k9, yo, k1. (25 sts)

Row 21: P11, yo, sl 2, k1, p2sso, yo, p11.

Row 22: K1, yo, k23, yo, k1. (27 sts)

Row 23: Purl.

Row 24: K1, yo, k25, yo, k1. (29 sts)

Row 25: P1, * yo, p2tog, rep from * across.

Row 26: K1, yo, k27, yo, k1. (31 sts)

Row 27: Purl.

Row 28: K1, yo, k29, yo, k1. (33 sts)

Row 29: P1, *yo, p2tog, rep from * across.

Row 30: K1, yo, k31, yo, k1. (35 sts)

Row 31: Purl.

Bind off all sts loosely.

Finishing

Join 4 triangles tog into a square. Sew 4 squares into a row to make 6 columns of squares. With crochet hook, work 1 rnd of reverse sc (crab st).

Block afghan to size. ◆

Garden Path

Design by Barbara Venishnick

Create the look of cobblestones while working from side to side! The fringe is created by cutting the yarn at the beginning and end of each main-color row.

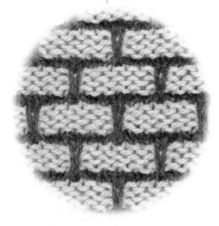

Pattern Notes

Afghan is worked from side to side. Entire length is cast on and afghan is worked across its width.

Fringe is made as you work. At beg and end of every color B row, leave a 6-inch tail; gather tails tog after every 4 row color B sequence and tie in a knot.

Sl all sts purlwise with yarn on WS of fabric.

Afghan

With A, cast on 161 sts.

Row 1 (RS): Knit.

Row 2: Purl.

Rows 3 and 4: With B, k2, *sl 1, k5, rep from * to last 3 sts, end sl 1, k2.

Row 5: With B, p2, *sl 1, p5, rep from * to last 3 sts, end sl 1, p2.

Row 6: Rep Row 3.

Rows 7 and 8: Rep Rows 1 and 2.

Skill Level

Advanced Beginner**

Finished Size

Approximately 39 x 54 inches

Materials

- Plymouth Encore Chunky bulky weight 75 percent acrylic/25 percent wool yarn (143 yds/100g per ball): 4 balls gray heather #389 (A), 7 balls beige heather #240 (B)
- Size 11 (8mm) 29-inch circular needle or size needed to obtain gauge
- Tapestry needle

Gauge

12 sts and 23 rows = 4 inches/ 10cm in pat

To save time, take time to check gauge.

Rows 9 and 10: With B, *k5, sl 1, rep from * to last 5 sts, end k5.

Row 11: With B, *p5, sl 1, rep from * to last 5 sts, end p5.

Row 12: Rep Row 9.

[Rep Rows 1–12] 17 more times, then [rep Rows 1–8] once more.

With A, bind off purlwise on RS.

Finishing

Block lightly and trim fringe as needed. ◆

Lace & Lavender

Design by Kathleen Power Johnson

A delicate square afghan worked in the round is enhanced by a border of tiny buds.

Skill Level

Intermediate***

Finished Size

Approximately 38 inches square

Materials

- Plymouth Encore worsted weight 75 percent acrylic/25 percent wool yarn (200 yds/100g per ball): 4 balls natural #256 (A), 1 ball each lilac #233 (B), green #1231 (C)
- Size 8 (5mm) set of 5 double-pointed needles and 24- and 36-inch circular needles or size needed to obtain gauge
- Stitch markers (optional)
- Size G/6 (4mm) crochet hook
- Tapestry needle

Gauge

16 sts and 24 rows = 4 inches/10cm in pat

To save time, take time to check gauge.

Pattern Notes

Beg working on dpns, changing to circular needles as work progresses. Use st markers to separate 4 sections, using a different color to mark beg of rnd.

Rep each line of instructions on each of 4 dpns or in each of 4 sections on circular needle.

Special Abbreviations

Cdd (Central double decrease): Sl next 2 sts as if to k2tog, k1, p2sso.

Pattern Stitches

Double throw: Wrap yarn twice around needle when forming k st.

4-throw: Wrap yarn 4 times around needle between sts.

Make bud: [K1, p1, k1, p1, k1] in next st, [turn and k5] 3 times, turn and work a double throw into each st. *(KnitTip: Cut lilac yarn into 24-inch lengths for buds)*

Afghan

To cast on: With A, make a sl knot. With tail at bottom, *insert crochet hook into loop of knot, wrap yarn around hook and pull loop through; wrap yarn once more and pull through loop on hook; rep from * 7 more times for 8 cast on sts. (Pull tail later to tighten cast on rnd.) Divide sts evenly on 4 needles.

Rnd 1 and all odd-numbered rnds: Knit.

Rnd 2: K1, yo, k1.

Rnd 4: [K1, yo] twice, k1.

Rnd 6: K1, yo, k3, yo, k1.

Rnd 8: K1, yo, k5, yo, k1.

Rnd 10: K1, yo, k7, yo, k1.

Rnd 12: K1, yo, k9, yo, k1.

Rnd 14: K1, yo, k11, yo, k1.

Rnd 16: K1, yo, k13, yo, k1.

Rnd 18: K1, yo, k15, yo, k1.

Rnd 20: [K1, yo] twice, k5, k2tog, k1, ssk, k5, [yo, k1] twice. (21 sts)

Rnd 22: [K1, yo] twice, k2tog, yo, k4, k2tog, k1, ssk, k4, yo, ssk, [yo, k1] twice.

Rnd 24: [K1, yo] twice, [k2tog, yo] twice, k3, k2tog, k1, ssk, k3, [yo, ssk] twice, [yo, k1] twice.

Rnd 26: [K1, yo] twice, [k2tog, yo] 3 times, k2, k2tog, k1, ssk, k2, [yo, ssk] 3 times, [yo, k1] twice.

Rnd 28: [K1, yo] twice, [k2tog, yo] 4 times, k1, k2tog, k1, ssk, k1, [yo, ssk] 4 times, [yo, k1] twice.

Rnd 30: [K1, yo] twice, [k2tog, yo] 5 times, k2tog, k1, ssk, [yo, ssk] 5 times, [yo, k1] twice. (31 sts)

Rnd 32: [K1, yo] twice, [k2tog, yo] 6 times, cdd, [yo, ssk] 6 times, [yo, k1] twice.

Rnd 34: [K1, yo] twice, [k2tog, yo] 6 times, k2tog, k1, ssk, [yo, ssk] 6 times, [yo, k1] twice.

Rnd 36: [K1, yo] twice, [k2tog, yo] 7 times, cdd, [yo, ssk] 7 times, [yo, k1] twice.

Rnd 38: [K1, yo] twice, [k2tog, yo] 7 times, k2tog, k1, ssk, [yo, ssk] 7 times, [yo, k1] twice.

Rnd 40: [K1, yo] twice, [k2tog, yo] 8 times, cdd, [yo, ssk] 8 times, [yo, k1] twice. (41 sts)

Rnd 42: [K1, yo] twice, [k2tog, yo] 8 times, k2tog, k1, ssk, [yo, ssk] 8 times, [yo, k1] twice.

Rep Rnds 40–43, inc reps by 1 every 4th rnd as established. Continue until Rnd 118 (there will be 119 sts in each section).

Border

Rnd 119: Knit.

Rnd 120: K1, yo, k 117, yo, k1. (121 sts)

Rnd 121: Knit.

Rnd 122: K1, yo, k119, yo, k1. (123 sts)

Rnd 123: Knit.

Rnd 124: K1, yo, k5, *attach strand of B and work bud, with A, k9, rep from * across section, ending last rep

Continued on page 38

Climbing Roses

Design by Sheryl McBreen

This afghan was inspired by a garden lattice with climbing roses. The three-dimensional roses and leaves add a beautiful finishing touch.

Skill Level
Advanced Beginner**

Finished Size
Approximately 46 x 66 inches

Materials
- Plymouth Encore worsted weight 75 percent acrylic/25 percent wool yarn (200 yds/100g per ball): 11 balls natural #256 (MC), 1 ball dark rose #180 (A), 2 balls light rose #9408 (B), 3 balls medium green #1232 (C), 4 balls light green #1231 (D)
- Size 8 (5mm) needles or size needed to obtain gauge
- Tapestry needle

Gauge
16 sts and 24 rows = 4 inches/ 10cm in diamond lattice pat

To save time, take time to check gauge.

Special Abbreviation
Cdd (Central double decrease): Sl next 2 sts as if to k2tog, k1, p2sso.

Pattern Stitches
Diamond Lattice Pat (multiple of 8 sts + 2)

Row 1: K1, *p1, k7, rep from * to last st, k1.

Row 2: P1, *k1, p5, k1, p1, rep from * to last st, p1.

Rows 3 and 7: K1, *k2, p1, k3, p1, k1, rep from * to last st, k1.

Rows 4 and 6: P1, *p2, k1, p1, k1, p3, rep from * to last st, p1.

Row 5: K1, *k4, p1, k3, rep from * to last st, k1.

Row 8: P1, *k1, p5, k1, p1, rep from * to last st, p1.

Rep Rows 1–8 for pat.

Edging Pat

Cast on 6 sts.

Row 1: P2, yo, k2tog, yo, k2. (7 sts)

Rows 2, 4, 6, 8 and 10: Knit.

Row 3: P2, k1, yo, k2tog, yo, k2. (8 sts)

Row 5: P2, k2, yo, k2tog, yo, k2. (9 sts)

Row 7: P2, k3, yo, k2tog, yo, k2. (10 sts)

Row 9: P2, k4, yo, k2tog, yo, k2. (11 sts)

Row 11: Bind off 6, yo, k2tog, yo, k2. (6 sts remaining)

Row 12: Knit.

Rep Rows 1–12 for pat.

Afghan Panel
Make 3

With MC, cast on 58 sts.

Row 1: Knit.

Row 2: Purl.

Beg diamond lattice pat and work until piece measures approximately 58 inches, ending with Row 1 of pat.

Purl 1 row, and bind off all sts.

Sew panels tog.

Edging
With MC, beg edging pat and rep Rows 1–12 until piece is needed length, ending with Row 12. K5, then bind off. Make 2 (58-inch) pieces and 2 (42-inch) pieces.

Sew borders to afghan.

Rose
Make 18 each with A and B

Cast on 31 sts.

Rows 1 and 3: *K1, p1, rep from * across.

Rows 2 and 4: *P1, k1, rep from * across.

Bind off all sts, leaving a long tail for sewing.

Leaf
Make 19 each with C and D

Cast on 3 sts.

Row 1: Knit.

Row 2 and remaining WS rows: Purl.

Row 3: K1, yo, k1, yo, k1.

Row 5: K2, yo, k1, yo, k2.

Row 7: K3, yo, k1, yo, k3.

Row 9: Knit.

Row 11: K3, cdd, k3.

Row 13: K2, cdd, k2.

Row 15: K1, cdd, k1.

Row 17: Cdd. Fasten off last st.

Referring to Fig. 1 (page 39) for placement, sew roses and leaves in corners. Sew all color A roses with color C leaves and all color B roses with color D leaves. Sew on roses by beg at center of rose and twirling it around itself, sewing through cast on edge as you twirl. Pull other yarn end through to back.

Sew leaves in place by catching 1 loop of edge st all around. Pull other yarn end through to back. Please don't worry if roses and leaves aren't all evenly spaced—they don't grow that way in nature! ◆

Figure 1 on page 39

Country Garden Mosaic

Design by Jacqueline W. Hoyle

Mosaic slip stitch is a wonderful way for the beginner to enjoy the look of color work without stranding.

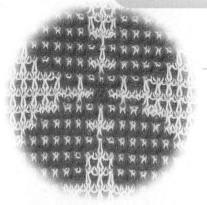

Skill Level
Advanced Beginner**

Finished Measurements
Approximately 33 x 59 inches

Materials
- Plymouth Encore worsted weight 75 percent acrylic/25 percent wool yarn (200 yds/100g per ball): 3 balls white #208 (MC), 1 ball each dark raspberry #1607 (A), dark rose #180 (B), light rose #9408 (C), 2 balls dark spruce #1604 (D)
- Size 15 (10mm) 24-inch circular needle or size needed to obtain gauge
- Row counter (optional)
- Tapestry needle

Gauge
12 sts and 22 rows = 4 inches/10cm in mosaic pat

To save time, take time to check gauge.

Pattern Notes
Each garter st block, forms a square 53 sts wide by 102 rows high. Each chart row represents 2 rows of knitting, a RS row and following WS row. In mosaic knitting, these 2 rows are alike, and are both worked on the same sts with the same strand of yarn. RS rows, beg with an odd number at RH edge of charts, work from right to left. WS rows (even number at LH edge of chart on same line) bring same color back to RH edge of knitting, where it can be exchanged for other color.

RS rows beg at RH edge of chart with alternate black and white squares. These squares represent first st of each row at RH edge of knitting. On every RS row beg with a black square, k all black sts in color A, B, or C and sl all white (MC) sts purlwise, with yarn in back. On every RS row beg with a white square, k all white sts and sl all black sts purlwise with yarn in back. WS rows are worked with yarn held in front (on WS of fabric) as sts are sl.

Body
With MC, cast on 53 sts. Knit 1 row.

Rows 1 and 2: Attach A, k all sts across.

Row 3: With MC, k1, sl 1 A st, with MC k across row to last 2 sts, sl 1 A st, k 1 MC st.

Row 4: Rep Row 3.

Work Rows 5–102 from Mosaic Chart (page 38). Knit 2 rows MC, bind off all sts on next row.

Work 1 more square with same colors.

Work 2 squares with MC and B and 2 squares with MC and C.

Referring to photo, sew squares tog by picking up garter st loops of each color strip, matching stripes across seam, so that speckled edge sts are concealed and 2nd st vertical stripes form border between squares.

Finishing
With D, *pick up and k 1 st in each bind off st across bottom, 3 for every 4 sts along side of afghan, inc 2 sts at corner by [k1, yo, k1] in same st, rep from * across top and remaining side.

Knit 2 rows, finishing 4th corner.

I-Cord Edging
Work attached I-Cord as follows:

Cast on 3 sts on LH needle. *K2, k 3rd st and first st of afghan edging tog, using ssk. Return 3 sts to LH needle*. Work attached I-Cord for a total of 8 sts. Work 12 rounds of detached I-Cord (*k3, sl sts to other end of needle, rep from *). Remove 3 sts from RH needle and holding them between thumb and forefinger, twist cord clockwise 1 complete turn and return sts to RH needle. Attach at base of cord by k1 into bottom st at base of detached I-cord and between 7th and 8th sts of attached I-cord, treating them as 1 st. There are now 4 sts on your RH needle. Pass 2nd st from end of needle over first st and off needle. Transfer 3 remaining sts to LH needle and continue to work attached I-Cord across next 8 sts, then work detached I-Cord loop again*. Work between *'s to 3 corner sts. Work attached I-Cord into first st, work 1 rnd of detached I-Cord, attach I-Cord to middle st, work 1 round of detached I-Cord, attach to 3rd st. Continue attaching I-Cord to next 8 side sts and beg detached loops again. When all 4 sides are completed, fasten off and sew end to beg. ◆

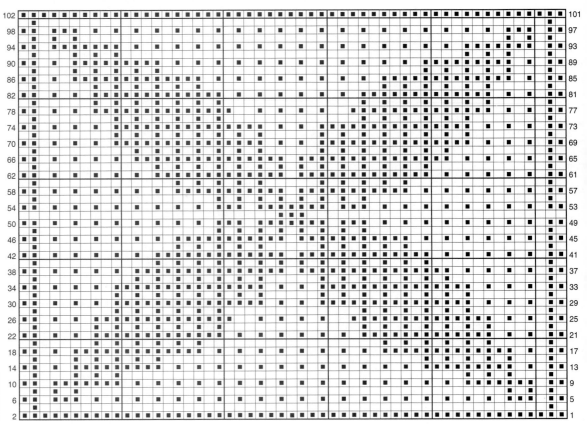

MOSAIC CHART

COLOR KEY
☐ MC
■ CC

Lace & Lavender continued from page 32

k5, yo, k1. (125 sts)

Rnd 125: K7, *sl 5 purlwise dropping extra strands, k9, rep from * across section, ending last rep k7.

Rnd 126: With C, k1, yo, k6, *k5tog, k9, rep from * across section, ending last rep k6, yo, k1. (127 sts)

Rnd 127: With C, p8, *4-throw, p1, 4-throw, p9, rep from * across section, ending last rep p8.

Rnd 128: With A, k1, yo, k7, *drop 4-throw to front of work, k1, drop 4-throw to front of work, k9, rep from * across section, ending last rep k7, yo, k1. (129 sts)

To tie bows: pull loops up tightly with needle tip and tie tog in square knot.

Rnd 129: Knit.

Rnd 130: K1, yo, k127, yo, k1. (131 sts)

Rnd 131: Purl.

Rnd 132: K1, yo, k129, yo, k1. (133 sts)

Rnd 133: Purl.

Rnd 134: K1, yo, k130, yo, k1. (135 sts)

Rnd 135: Bind off all sts purlwise.

Finishing

Gently wet or steam block. ◆

Climbing Roses continued from page 34

FIG. 1

Lap Warmers

*K*eep your legs cozy and comfortable with these six handsome throws. Toss one in the car when you're traveling and keep another close by your special chair for watching television. A special wheelchair-sized throw with a pocket is included in this collection.

Chapter 3

Dad's Drop-Stitch Throw

Design by Edie Eckman

Openwork stripes and garter stitch make this a great beginner afghan. Knit on size 13 needles with no finishing, it's a quick-to-knit throw that will please any gentleman.

Skill Level
Beginner*

Finished Size
Approximately 45 x 60 inches

Materials
- Plymouth Encore Colorspun worsted weight 75 percent acrylic/25 percent wool yarn (200 yds/100g per ball): 11 balls tweed #7172
- Size 13 (9mm) 29- or 36-inch circular needle or size needed to obtain gauge
- Tapestry needle

Gauge
10 sts and 14 rows = 4 inches/10cm in patt

To save time, take time to check gauge.

Pattern Notes
Use 2 strands of yarn throughout.

Check length of afghan by holding it vertically; weight of afghan will make it stretch.

Afghan
Cast on 113 sts.

Rows 1–4: Knit.

Row 5: Knit, wrapping yarn around needle twice on each st.

Row 6: Knit, dropping extra wrap from each st.

Rep Rows 1–6 until piece measures approximately 60 inches, ending with Row 4 of pat.

Bind off all sts loosely. ◆

Autumn Lace Lap Warmer

Design by Fatema Rahman

Curl up with a good book and a cup of tea under this allover lace lap afghan. When the autumn evenings get frosty, it'll keep you toasty warm.

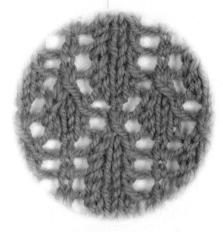

Skill Level
Easy**

Finished Size
Approximately 35 x 45 inches

Materials
- Plymouth Encore worsted weight 75 percent acrylic/25 percent wool yarn (200 yds/100g per ball): 4 balls sage green #1232
- Size 10 (6mm) 24-inch circular needle or size needed to obtain gauge
- Stitch markers
- Tapestry needle

Gauge
18 sts and 20 rows = 4 inches/10cm in pat

To save time, take time to check gauge.

Pattern Stitch
Autumn Lace St (multiple of 6 sts + 1)

Row 1 and remaining WS rows: Purl.

Rows 2, 4, and 6: K1, *yo, ssk, k1, k2tog, yo, k1, rep from * across.

Row 8: K2, * yo, sl 1, k2 tog, psso, yo, k3, rep from *, end last rep k2 instead of k3.

Row 10: K1, *k2tog, yo, k1, yo, ssk, k1, rep from * across.

Row 12: K2tog, *yo, k3, yo, sl 1, k2tog, psso, rep from *, end yo, k3, yo, ssk.

Rep Rows 1–12 for pat.

Afghan
Cast on 129 sts. Work 6 rows in garter st.

Beg pat

Row 1: K4, pm, work Row 1 of pat across to last 4 sts, pm, k4.

Work in pat, keeping 4 border sts at each edge in garter st throughout until piece measures 44 inches from beg. Work 6 sts rows of garter st. Bind off all sts loosely.

Finishing
Wet block severely. ◆

Raspberry Afghan

Design by Shari Haux

Twisted rib stripes work up into a unique and elegant afghan. Knit in dark raspberry yarn, it would also make a great Christmas afghan.

Afghan

Cast on 258 sts. Knit 10 rows.

Beg pat

Row 1 (RS): K6, pm, p4, *k1tbl, [p1, k1tbl] 3 times, p4, rep from * to last 6 sts, end k6.

Row 2: K6, k4, *p1, [k1tbl, p1] 3 times, k4, rep from * to last 6 sts, end k6.

Rep Rows 1 and 2 until piece measures approximately 61½ inches from beg.

Knit 10 rows. Bind off all sts. ◆

Skill Level

Beginner*

Finished Size

Approximately 58 x 63 inches

Materials

- Plymouth Encore worsted weight 75 percent acrylic/25 percent wool yarn (200 yds/100g per ball): 12 balls dark raspberry #1607
- Size 8 (5mm) needles or size needed to obtain gauge
- Stitch markers
- Tapestry needle

Gauge

18 sts and 24 rows = 4 inches/10cm in pat

To save time, take time to check gauge.

Diamonds Light & Lofty

Design by Ann E. Smith

This afghan is a charming way for the beginner to appreciate the contrast between garter and stockinette stitch. What a great beginner project!

Skill Level
Beginner*

Finished Size
Approximately 40 x 50 inches, excluding fringe

Materials
- Plymouth Encore Chunky bulky weight 75 percent acrylic/25 percent wool yarn (143 yds/100g per ball): 10 balls beige heather #240
- Size 11 (8mm) needles or size needed to obtain gauge
- Tapestry needle
- Crochet hook

Gauge
12 sts and 17 rows = 4 inches/10cm in pat

To save time, take time to check gauge.

Afghan
Beg at lower edge, cast on 121 sts.

Row 1 (WS): K3, p115, k3.

Row 2: Knit.

Body Pat (multiple of 22 sts + 33)

Row 1 (WS): K3, p7, *k13, p4, k1, p4, rep from * across, end k13, p7, k3.

Row 2 and all RS rows: Knit.

Row 3: K3, p8, *k11, p4, k3, p4, rep from * across, end k11, p8, k3.

Row 5: K3, p9, *k9, p4, k5, p4, rep from * across, end k9, p9, k3.

Row 7: K3, p10, *k7, p4, k7, p4, rep from * across, end k7, p10, k3.

Row 9: K3, p11, *k5, p4, k9, p4, rep from * across, end k5, p11, k3.

Row 11: K3, p12, *k3, p4, k11, p4, rep from * across, end k3, p12, k3.

Row 13: K3, p13, *k1, p4, k13, p4, rep from * across, end k1, p13, k3.

Row 15: Rep Row 11.

Row 17: Rep Row 9.

Row 19: Rep Row 7.

Row 21: Rep Row 5.

Row 23: Rep Row 3.

Row 24: Knit.

Rep Rows 1–24 for pat until piece measures approximately 50 inches from beg, ending with Row 13 or Row 1.

Knit 1 row.

Next row: K3, p115, k3.

Bind off all sts loosely and knitwise.

Fringe
Cut 1 (60-inch) strand, fold in half three times (top fold forms a loop). With WS of afghan facing, insert crochet hook through first st at corner, pull loop through st, thread ends through and pull up to form a knot. Make a fringe for every other st across lower and upper edges. Do not cut loops. ◆

STITCH KEY
☐ K on RS, p on WS
⊟ K on WS

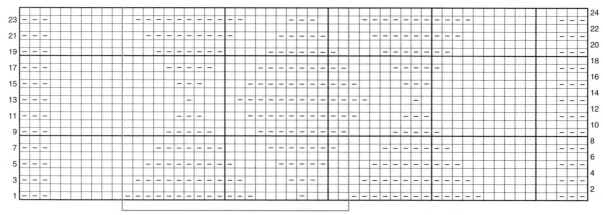

Rep

CHART A

Northern Lights

Design by Barbara Venishnick

Enjoy the luxury of combining fibers with this quick-to-knit throw. Worked with size 17 needles, the four strands held together throughout create a dazzling effect.

Pattern Stitch

(Multiple of 6 sts + 3)

Row 1 and remaining RS rows: Knit.

Row 2: Knit.

Rows 4 and 6: P3, *k3, p3, rep from * across.

Rows 8 and 10: Knit.

Rows 12 and 14: K3, *p3, k3, rep from * across.

Row 16: Knit.

Rep Rows 1–16 for pat.

Pattern Notes

Afghan is worked with 1 strand of each of 4 yarns held tog throughout.

Circular needle is used to accomodate large number of sts. Do not join, work back and forth in rows.

Afghan

Cast on 87 sts. Work in pat until 11 reps of pat are completed. Rep [Rows 1–10] once. Bind off all sts.

Fringe

Each fringe is made up of 2 strands each of A, B and C, and 1 strand of D (7 strands). Cut strands 10 inches long.

Working across ends, beg at right edge, *insert crochet hook in st from back to front, fold fringe in half and pull loop through to back. Pull tails of fringe through loop formed at middle. Pull tight to secure. Skip 2 sts and and rep from *, placing a fringe in every 3rd st across both ends. ◆

Skill Level

Beginner*

Finished Size

45 x 60 inches

Materials

- Plymouth Encore worsted weight 75 percent acrylic/25 percent wool yarn (200 yds/100g per ball): 5 balls flecked burgundy #560 (A)
- Cleckheaton Mohair 12-ply 92 percent mohair/4 percent wool/4 percent nylon yarn (110 yds/50g per ball) from Plymouth Yarns: 9 balls black #213 (B)
- Indiecita Alpaca Boucle bulky weight 87 percent alpaca/13 percent nylon yarn (115 yds/50g per ball) from Plymouth Yarns: 9 balls multicolor #112 (C)
- Gold Rush sport weight 80 percent rayon/20 percent metallised polyester yarn (110 yds/25g per cone) from Plymouth Yarns: 9 cones burgundy #40 (D)
- Size 17 (12.5mm) 29-inch circular needle or size needed to obtain gauge
- Size G/6 (4mm) crochet hook (for attaching fringe)
- Tapestry needle

Gauge

8 sts and 12 rows = 4 inches/10cm in pat with 4 strands of yarn held tog

To save time, take time to check gauge.

Sumptuous Stripes Afghan

Design by Lois S. Young

A simple but clever way to achieve vertical stripes is to work sideways! Alternating wide and narrow stripes with stockinette stitch adds interest to the design.

Skill Level
Beginner*

Finished Size
Approximately 40 x 50 inches

Materials
- Cleckheaton 12 ply Mohair 92 percent mohair/4 percent wool/4 percent nylon yarn (110 yds/100g per ball) from Plymouth Yarns: 7 skeins butterscotch #251 (MC)
- Plymouth Encore worsted weight 75 percent acrylic/25 percent wool yarn (200 yds/100g per ball): 1 ball ecru #218 (CC)
- Size 9 (5.5mm) 29-inch circular needle or size needed to obtain gauge
- Tapestry needle

Gauge
14 sts = 4 inches/10 cm in St st, 13 rows = 2.5 inches

To save time, take time to check gauge.

Pattern Notes
Throw is worked sideways so that the stripes will be vertical when throw is used.

Sl first st of each knit row as if to p and each purl row as if to k so that a ch of sts runs up selvages of throw.

When changing colors, work last st of row before color change in new color.

Pattern Stitches
Wide Stripes

Row 1 (WS): With MC, knit.

Rows 2–5: With CC, knit.

Rows 6–8: With MC, knit.

Row 9: With MC, purl.

Row 10: With MC, knit.

Rows 11–20: Rep Rows 1–10.

Rows 21–27: Rep Rows 1–7.

Narrow Stripe

Row 1 (WS): With MC, knit.

Rows 2 and 3: With CC, knit.

Rows 4 and 5: With MC, knit.

Throw
With MC, loosely cast on 156 sts.

Knit 6 rows.

Work 5 rows St st, ending with a RS row.

[Work wide stripes, work 13 rows St st in MC, work narrow stripe, work 13 rows St st in MC] 3 times.

Work wide stripes.

Work 5 rows St st in MC.

Knit 6 rows with MC for border. Bind off knitwise on WS.

Edging for Top and Bottom
With MC and RS of throw facing you, pick up and k sts along chained edge of throw at a rate of 3 sts for every 4 rows: *pick up 1 st from chained loop of selvage, pick up st from next ch, yo, rep from *. (approximately 164 sts)

Knit 6 rows. Bind off knitwise on WS.

Finishing
Block by pinning to size on carpet. Mist with water from spray bottle, let dry. ◆

Herringbone Pie Throw

Design by Jill Wolcott

Instead of dividing into quarters, join these quarters to make a whole. Simple color changes make interesting circular stripes.

Skill Level
Intermediate***

Finished Measurements
Approximately 36-inch diameter

Materials
- Plymouth Encore worsted weight 75 percent acrylic/25 percent wool yarn (200 yds/100g per ball): 3 balls each plum #2426 (A), mauve #433 (B)
- Size 8 (5mm) double-pointed (set of 5) and 24-inch circular needles or size needed to obtain gauge
- Stitch markers
- Stitch holders or waste yarn
- Crochet hook (for finishing)
- Tapestry needle

Gauge
16 sts and 22 rows = 4 inches/10cm in St st

To save time, take time to check gauge.

Special Abbreviations
K1below: Following a purl st: k into top of st below next st on left needle (inc 1). Before a purl st: k into top of st below st just knitted (inc 1).

Afghan St: Drop first st on each of 2 adjoining edges down to cast-on row. With a latch hook or crochet hook, from RS, put hook into 1 loop and draw up 1 loop from adjacent edge; rep once, then grab 2 loops on alternate edges, pulling through first 2 loops, continue up to last row. Temporarily place remaining loops on st holder or waste yarn. Rep on remaining edges to form circular piece.

P3tog: Purl 3 sts tog. (dec 2 sts)

Pattern Note
Afghan is worked in quarters which are joined to form the whole.

Edge
Cast on 142 sts, using long-tail cast on and both colors: hold yarn with Color B over thumb and Color A over index finger.

With A, knit 2 rows. Cut A, with B, knit 2 rows. Work pattern sequence below.

Body
Rows 1–12: Use color A.

Row 1 (RS): P2, *k1below, k10, p5, p3tog, p5, k10, k1below, p2, rep from * across. (142 sts)

Row 2 and all remaining WS rows not given: K the knit sts and p the purl sts.

Row 3: P2, *k1below, k11, p4, p3tog, p4, k11, k1below, p2, rep from * across.

Row 5: P2, *k1below, k12, p3, p3tog, p3, k12, k1below, p2, rep from * across.

Row 7: P2, *k1below, k13, p2, p3tog, p2, k13, k1below, p2, rep from * across.

Row 9: P2, *k1below, k14, p1, p3tog, p1, k14, k1below, p2, rep from * across.

Row 11: P2, *k15, p3tog, k15, p2, rep from * across. (134 sts)

Rows 13–24: Use color B.

Row 13: P2, *k1below, k9, p5, p3tog,
p5, k9, k1below, p2, rep from * across.

Row 15: P2, *k1below, k10, p4, p3tog, p4, k10, k1below, p2, rep from * across.

Row 17: P2, *k11, p3, p3tog, p3, k11, p2, rep from * across. (126 sts)

Row 19: P2, *k1below, k11, p2, p3tog, p2, k11, k1below, p2, rep from * across.

Row 21: P2, *k1below, k12, p1, p3tog, p1, k12, k1below, p2, rep from * across.

Row 23: P2, *k13, p3tog, k13, p2, rep from * across. (118 sts)

Rows 25–36: Use color A.

Row 25: P2, *k1below, k7, p5, p3tog, p5, k7, k1below, p2, rep from * across.

Row 27: P2, *k1below, k8, p4, p3tog, p4, k8, k1below, p2, rep from * across.

Row 29: P2, *k9, p3, p3tog, p3, k9, p2, rep from * across. (110 sts)

Row 31: P2, *k1below, k9, p2, p3tog, p2, k9, k1below, p2, rep from * across.

Row 33: P2, *k1below, k10, p1, p3tog, p1, k10, k1below, p2, rep from * across.

Row 35: P2, *k11, p3tog, k11, p2, rep from * across. (102 sts)

Rows 37–46: Use color B.

Row 37: P2, *k1below, k6, p4, p3tog, p4, k6, k1below, p2, rep from * across.

Row 39: P2, *k1below, k7, p3, p3tog, p3, k7, k1below, p2, rep from * across.

Row 41: P2, *k8, p2, p3tog, p2, k8, p2, rep from * across. (94 sts)

Row 43: P2, *k1below, k8, p1, p3tog,

p1, k8, k1below, p2.

Row 45: P2, *k1below, k9, p3tog, k9, k1below, p2, rep from * across.

Rows 47–56: Use color A.

Row 47: P2, *k5, p4, p3tog, p4, k5, p2, rep from * across. (86 sts)

Row 49: P2, *k1below, k5, p3, p3tog, p3, k5, k1below, p2, rep from * across.

Row 51: P2, *k1below, k6, p2, p3tog, p2, k6, k1below, p2, rep from * across.

Row 53: P2, *k7, p1, p3tog, p1, k7, p2, rep from * across. (78 sts)

Row 55: P2, *k1below, k7, p3tog, k7, k1below, p2, rep from * across.

Rows 57–66: Use color B.

Row 57: P2, *k1below, k3, p4, p3tog, p4, k3, k1below, p2, rep from * across.

Row 59: P2, *k4, p3, p3tog, p3, k4, p2, rep from * across. (70 sts)

Row 61: P2, *k1below, k4, p2, p3tog, p2, k4, k1below, p2, rep from * across.

Row 63: P2, *k1below, k5, p1, p3tog, p1, k5, k1below, p2, rep from * across.

Row 65: P2, *k6, p3tog, k6, p2, rep from * across. (62 sts)

Rows 67–74: Use color A.

Row 67: P2, *k1below, k2, p3, p3tog, p3, k2, k1below, p2, rep from * across.

Row 69: P2, *k1below, k3, p2, p3tog, p2, k3, k1below, p2, rep from * across.

Row 71: P2, *k4, p1, p3tog, p1, k4, p2, rep from * across. (54 sts)

Row 73: P2, *k1below, k4, p3tog, k4, k1below, p2, rep from * across.

Rows 75–80: Use color B.

Row 75: P2, *k1below, k2, p2, p3tog, p2, k2, k1below, p2, rep from * across.

Row 77: P2, *k3, p1, p3tog, p1, k3, p2, rep from * across. (46 sts)

Row 79: P2, *k1below, k3, p3tog, k3, k1below, p2, rep from * across.

Rows 81–86: Use color A.

Row 81: P2, *k1below, k1, p2, p3tog, p2, k1, k1below, p2, rep from * across.

Row 83: P2, *k2, p1, p3tog, p1, k2, p2, rep from * across. (38 sts)

Row 85: P2, *k1below, k2, p3tog, k2, k1below, p2, rep from * across.

Rows 87–90: Use color B.

Row 87: P2, *k1below, k1, p1, p3tog, p1, k1, k1below, p2, rep from * across.

Row 89: P2, *k1below, k2, p3tog, k2, k1below, p2.

Rows 91–94: Use color A.

Row 91: P2, *k1below, k1, p1, p3tog, p1, k1, k1below, p2, rep from * across.

Row 93: P2, *k1below, k2, p3tog, k2, k1below, p2, rep from * across.

Rows 95–98: Use color B.

Row 95: P2, *k1, p1, p3tog, p1, k1, p2, rep from * across. (30 sts)

Row 97: P2, *k1, p3tog, k1, p2, rep from * across. (22 sts)

Rows 99–101: Use color A.

Row 99: P2, *p3tog, p2, rep from * across. (14 sts)

Row 100: *K2, p1, rep from * across, end k2.

Row 101: P3, p3tog, p2, p3tog, p3. (10 sts)

Rows 102 and 103: Use color B.

Row 102: K2, p6, k2.

Row 103: P2, [p2tog, p2] twice. (8 sts)

Place remaining sts on holder. Rep for remaining 3 quarters.

Finishing

Weave in ends, working away from edge st so that it can be undone for afghan st. Join 3 seams using afghan st above. Return 29 sts to needles. Work as follows:

With B:

Row 1: K1, k2tog, k23, k2tog, k1. (27 sts)

Row 2: K2, *k2tog, k1, rep from * across, end k1. (19 sts)

With A:

Rows 3 and 4: Knit.

Row 5: K2, *K1, k3tog, k1, rep from *, end k2. (13 sts)

With B:

Row 7: Knit.

Row 8: K1, [k3tog] across to last 3 sts, end k2tog, k1. (6 sts)

Cut yarn. Join last seam using afghan st above. With tapestry needle, run yarn end through remaining sts twice. ◆

Wheelchair Throw

Design by Jacqueline W. Hoyle

Lace, cables and I-cord combined with pockets make this throw practical as well as pleasing. It's a great size to use with a wheelchair!

Skill Level

Intermediate***

Finished Size

Approximately 40 x 45 inches

Materials

- Plymouth Encore Colorspun worsted weight 75 percent acrylic/25 percent wool yarn (200 yds/100g per ball): 5 skeins rosy tweed #7990 (MC), 1 skein light raspberry #999 (CC)
- Size 9 (5.5mm) 24-inch circular needle
- Size 11 (8mm) 24-inch circular needle or size needed to obtain gauge
- Row counter
- Cable needle
- Stitch markers
- Tapestry needle

Gauge

15 sts and 20 rows = 4 inches/ 10cm in lace/cable st on larger needles

To save time, take time to check

Special Abbreviation

Rdd (right double dec): Ssk, sl resulting st to LH needle, pass 2nd st over first st, return rem st to RH needle. (2 sts dec)

Pattern Stitches

Seed St (even number of sts)

Row 1: *K1, p1, rep from * across.

Row 2: *P1, k1, rep from * across.

Rep Rows 1 and 2 for pat.

Lace Pat with 12 Stitch Cable (panel of 31 sts)

Row 1: K2tog, [yo, k3, yo, rdd] twice, yo, k3, yo, k2tog, k3, sl3 sts to cn, hold in back, k3, k3 from cn, k3.

Row 2: P12, [k1, p1, k3, p1] 3 times, k1.

Row 3: K1, [yo, ssk, k1, k2tog, yo, k1] 3 times, k12.

Row 4: Rep Row 2.

Row 5: K1, [k1, yo, rdd, yo, k2] 3 times, [sl 3 sts to cn, hold in front, k3, k3 from cn] twice.

Row 6: P12, [k2, p1, k1, p1, k1] 3 times, k1.

Row 7: K1, [k2tog, yo, k1, yo, ssk, k1] 3 times; k12.

Row 8: Rep Row 6.

Rep Rows 1–8.

Throw

With MC and larger needles, cast on 148 sts. Work 10 rows of seed st.

Set up pat

Row 1 (RS): Work 6 sts in seed st, pm, *19 sts in lace pat from Chart A, pm, 24-st cable from Chart B, (12-st cable chart worked twice), pm, 19 sts in lace pat from Chart A*, pm, 12 cable sts from Chart B, pm, [rep between * *] once, pm, 6 sts in seed st.

Work in pat until afghan measures approximately 40 inches from beg.

Work in pat to first cable, bind off 24 sts, continue across row to next 24-st cable, bind off 24 sts, complete row.

Pocket Linings

Make 2

With CC and larger needles, cast on 26 sts and work in Chart B pat, keeping first and last sts in garter st (knit every row) for 6 inches. Leave sts on needle.

On next row (WS), work to beg of bound off sts. With WS of afghan facing WS of pocket lining, purl across lining sts. Continue across row, adding 2nd lining in same way. (RS of pocket lining shows on WS of afghan)

Continue in pat, working first and last sts of lining tog with first and last sts of cable section on next row for a smoother join. Work even until piece measures 43½ inches from beg. Work 10 rows of seed st, then bind off loosely in pat.

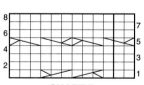

CHART A

CHART B

STITCH KEY
☐ K on RS, p on WS
⊟ P on RS, k on WS
◯ Yo
◲ K2tog
◺ Ssk
◸ Rdd
▷▷▷◁◁◁ Sl 3 sts to cn, hold in back, k3, k3 from cn
▷▷▷◁◁◁ Sl 3 sts to cn, hold in front, k3, k3 from cn

Pocket borders

With smaller needles and CC, pick up 24 bind off sts at top of pocket. Change to larger needles and work seed st border for 1 inch. Bind off all sts in pat. Rep for 2nd pocket.

Finishing

Pin linings to back of afghan and sl st in place. Sew ends of pocket borders in place.

Beg at bottom of throw with RS facing, work attached I-Cord in CC around outer edge as follows: with larger circular needle and CC, cast on 3 sts. Sl sts to other end of needle, k2, sl 1, yo, pick up and k 1 st in edge of throw. Sl yo and sl st on needle over k st and off needle. Sl remaining 3 sts on RH needle knitwise back to LH needle*. Rep between * *, picking up every st across bottom. After working 1 Corner st, work 1 rnd of free I-Cord: k3, sl sts to other end of needle, then resume between * *, attaching up side, working in 2 of every 3 rows. Work 1 rnd of free I-Cord at next corner, work all sts across top of throw, and 2 of every 3 rows down other side. Work last corner and across bottom to starting point. End by weaving or sewing ends tog, hiding ends inside cord. ◆

Little Snugglies

*W*hether you lovingly knit a cozy coverlet for your own precious little one or as a gift for a mother-to-be, there are few gifts as treasured as a hand-knitted baby afghan.

Chapter 4

Rainbow Blocks Baby Afghan

Design by Uyvonne Bigham

A delicate wave of color transforms simple blocks into a work of art. Instructions are given for knitting it in strips or knitting it in one piece.

Skill Level
Beginner*

Finished Size
Approximately 32 x 36 inches

Materials
- Plymouth Encore DK weight 75 percent acrylic/25 percent wool yarn (150 yds/50g per ball): 10 balls variegated pastels #7064
- Size 4 (3.5mm) needles
- Size 5 (3.75mm) needles or size needed to obtain gauge
- Tapestry needle

Gauge
24 sts = 4 inches/10cm in St st with larger needles

To save time, take time to check gauge.

Pattern Note
Instructions are given for making afghan in strips, followed by instructions for knitting it in one piece.

Afghan in Strips
Left Panel
Make 1

With smaller needles, cast on 51 sts and work 8 rows of garter st, ending with a WS row.

Change to larger needles and beg pat.

Left Block Pat
Row 1 (RS): Knit.

Row 2: [K6, p18] twice, k3.

Rows 3–20: Rep Rows 1 and 2.

Rows 21–26: Knit.

Rep Rows 1–26 for a total of 11 squares. [Rep Rows 1–20] once.

Change to smaller needles. Knit 8 rows. Bind off all sts.

Center Panels
Make 2

With smaller needles, cast on 48 sts and work 8 rows garter st, ending with a WS row.

Change to larger needles and beg pat.

Center Block Pat
Row 1 (RS): Knit.

Row 2: K3, p18, k6, p18, k3.

Rows 3–20: Rep Rows 1 and 2.

Rows 21–26: Knit.

Rep Rows 1–26 for a total of 11 squares. [Rep Rows 1–20] once.

Change to smaller needles. Knit 8 rows. Bind off all sts.

Right Panel
Make 1

With smaller needles, cast on 51 sts and work 8 rows garter st, ending with a WS row.

Change to larger needles and beg pat.

Right Block Pat
Row 1 (RS): Knit.

Row 2: K3, [p18, k6] twice.

Rows 3–20: Rep Rows 1 and 2.

Rows 21–26: Knit.

Rep Rows 1–26 for a total of 11 squares. [Rep Rows 1–20] once.

Change to smaller needles. Knit 8 rows. Bind off all sts.

Finishing
Sew center panels tog. Sew left and right panels to center panels with 6 st garter border at outside edge. Block lightly.

Afghan in One Piece
With smaller needles, cast on 198 sts and work 8 rows garter st, ending with a WS row.

Change to larger needles and beg pat.

Block Pat
Row 1 (RS): Knit.

Row 2: K6, *p18, k6, rep from * across.

Rows 3–20: Rep Rows 1 and 2.

Rows 21–26: Knit.

Rep Rows 1–26 for a total of 11 squares. [Rep Rows 1–20] once.

Change to smaller needles. Knit 8 rows. Bind off all sts.

Finishing
Block lightly. ◆

Warm & Cuddly Baby Afghan

Design by Uyvonne Bigham

Slip stitches and double strands combine to produce a two-toned thermal blanket. The garter stitch border eliminates the need for additional finishing.

Skill Level
Easy**

Finished Size
Approximately 32 x 36 inches

Materials
- Plymouth Encore DK weight 75 percent acrylic/25 percent wool yarn (150 yds/50g per ball): 6 balls aqua #1201 (MC), 5 balls white #208 (CC)
- Size 5 (3.75mm) needles
- Size 6 (4mm) needles or size needed to obtain gauge
- Stitch holders
- Tapestry needle

Gauge
18 sts = 4 inches/10cm in garter st with 2 strands of yarn and smaller needles

To save time, take time to check gauge.

Pattern Notes
Afghan is worked with 2 strands of yarn held tog throughout.

Sl all sts purlwise with yarn on WS of fabric.

For single color version, work pat as given, disregarding references to color changes.

Bottom Border
With smaller needles and 2 strands of MC, cast on 155 sts and work 13 rows of garter st.

Inc row: K11, then sl these sts to a holder for side border, k3, *inc in next st, k5, rep from * to last 12 sts, inc in next st, sl remaining 11 sts onto a holder for side border. (159 sts)

Beg pat
Change to larger needles, join CC and work in pat as follows:

Row 1 (RS): With CC, k1, sl 1, *k3, sl 1, rep from * to last st, end k1.

Row 2: With CC, k1, sl 1, *k3, sl 1, rep from * to last st, end k1.

Row 3: With MC, k3, *sl 1, k3, rep from * across.

Row 4: With MC, k3, *sl 1, k3, rep from * across.

Rep Rows 1–4 for pat until piece measures approximately 34½ inches from beg, ending with Row 2. Cut CC and sl all sts to a holder.

Left Side Border
Sl 11 sts on left edge to smaller needle with beg of row at inside edge (beg with a WS row). Join MC and work in garter st until band is same length as side edge, ending with a WS row. Sl sts to a holder.

Right Side Border
Sl 11 sts on right edge to smaller needle with beg of row at inside edge (beg with a RS row). Join MC and work border as for left border, ending with a WS row. Leave sts on needle.

Top Border
With smaller needles and MC, RS facing, k 11 sts of right border; work across center sts as follows: k2, k2tog, *k5, k2tog, rep from * to last 4 sts of center, k2tog, k2; k 11 sts of left border. (155 sts)

Work 14 rows of garter st. Bind off all sts.

Finishing
Sew side borders to center section. Block lightly. ◆

Butterfly Fantasy Baby Afghan

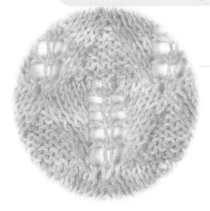

Design by Sue Childress

Drape your child in a field of butterflies with this quick-to-knit lace afghan. The changing colors of this beautiful yarn add to its delicate look.

Skill Level
Easy**

Finished Size
Approximately 42 x 46 inches

Materials
- Plymouth Encore Colorspun worsted weight 75 percent acrylic/25 percent wool yarn (200 yds/100g per ball): 6 balls pastels #7115
- Size 10 (6mm) needles or size needed to obtain gauge
- Tapestry needle

Gauge
16 sts = 4 inches/10cm in pat

To save time, take time to check gauge.

Afghan
Cast on 169 sts and knit 6 rows.

Beg pat
Row 1 (RS): K7, *yo, ssk, p7, k2tog, yo, k1, rep from * to last 6 sts, end k6.

Row 2: K6, p3, k7, *p5, k7, rep from * to last 9 sts, end p3, k6.

Row 3: K7, *yo, k1, ssk, p5, k2tog, k1, yo, k1, rep from * to last 6 sts, end k6.

Row 4: K6, p4, k5, *p7, k5, rep from * to last 10 sts, end p4, k6.

Row 5: K7, *yo, k2, ssk, p3, k2tog, k2, yo, k1, rep from * to last 6 sts, end k6.

Row 6: K6, p5, k3, *p9, k3, rep from * to last 11 sts, end p5, k6.

Row 7: K7, *yo, k3, ssk, p1, k2tog, k3, yo, k1, rep from * to last 6 sts, end k6.

Row 8: K6, p6, k1, *p11, k1, rep from * to last 12 sts, end p6, k6.

Row 9: K7, *yo, k4, sl 1, k2tog, psso, k4, yo, k1, rep from * to last 6 sts, end k6.

Row 10: K6, p to last 6 sts, end k6.

Row 11: K6, p4, k2tog, yo, k1, yo, ssk, *p7, k2tog, yo, k1, yo, ssk, rep from * to last 10 sts, end p4, k6.

Row 12: K10, p5, *k7, p5, rep from * to last 10 sts, end k10.

Row 13: K6, p3, k2tog, k1, [yo, k1] twice, ssk, *p5, k2tog, k1, [yo, k1] twice, ssk, rep from * to last 9 sts, end p3, k6.

Row 14: K9, p7, *k5, p7, rep from * to last 9 sts, end k9.

Row 15: K6, p2, k2tog, k2, yo, k1, yo, k2, ssk, *p3, k2tog, k2, yo, k1, yo, k2, ssk, rep from * to last 8 sts, end p2, k6.

Row 16: K8, p9, *k3, p9, rep from * to last 8 sts, end k8.

Row 17: K6, p1, *k2tog, k3, yo, k1, yo, k3, ssk, p1, rep from * to last 6 sts, end k6.

Row 18: K7, *p11, k1, rep from * to last 6 sts, end k6.

Row 19: K6, k2tog, k4, yo, k1, yo, k4, *sl 1, k2tog, psso, k4, yo, k1, yo, k4, rep from * to last 8 sts, end ssk, k6.

Row 20: K6, p to last 6 sts, end k6.

Rows 21–220: [Rep Rows 1–20] 10 more times.

Border
Knit 6 rows. Bind off all sts.

Block lightly. ◆

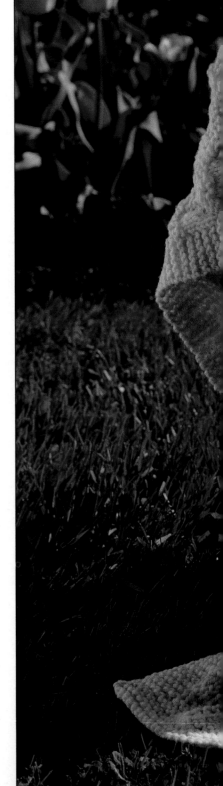

Rainbow Baby Afghan

Design by Nazanin S. Fard

The vertical lace pattern of this baby afghan is very beautiful, yet very easy to create. Colorspun, a worsted weight variegated, adds additional interest to this afghan.

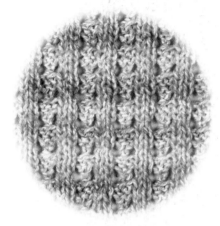

Skill Level
Intermediate***

Finished Size
Approximately 41 inches square

Materials
- Plymouth Encore Colorspun worsted weight 75 percent acrylic/25 percent wool yarn (200 yds/100g per ball): 7 balls variegated pastels #7065
- Size 8 (5mm) needles or size needed to obtain gauge
- Tapestry needle

Gauge
16 sts and 30 rows = 4 inches/10cm in St st

To save time, take time to check gauge.

Pattern Notes
Pat is a multiple of 3 sts + 1 + 3 border sts on each edge, inc to a multiple of 5 sts + 3 + 3 border sts on each edge. Original st count is restored on Row 4.

To make border lie flat, at beg and end of every 12th row, k3, turn, k3 (short row), then work row as established.

Pattern Stitch
Row 1: K3, *yo, k1, yo, p2, rep from *, end yo, k1, yo, k3. (264 sts)

Row 2: K3, *p3, k2, rep from * end p3, k3.

Row 3: K6, *p2, k3, rep from *, end k6.

Row 4: K3, *p3tog, k2, rep from *, end p3tog, k3. (160 sts)

Rep Rows 1–4 for pat.

Afghan
Cast on 160 sts. Knit 6 rows of garter st, then work in pat until afghan measures approximately 40 inches, ending with Row 4. Knit 6 rows of garter st. Bind off all sts loosely. ◆

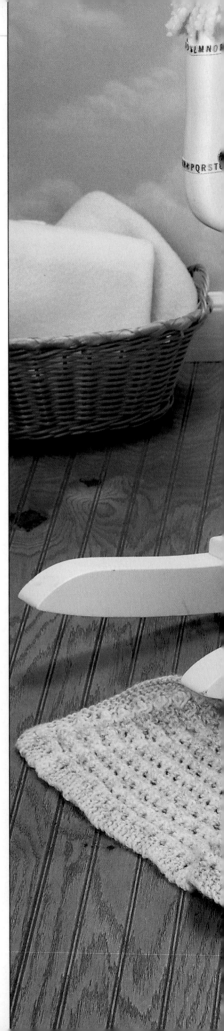

Little Huggy Baby Blanket

Design by Frances Hughes

Columns of lace and a seed-stitch border make up a delightful blanket. It's just the right size for cuddling your precious little one.

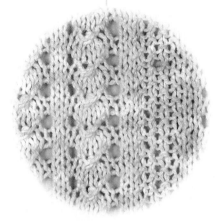

Skill Level
Intermediate***

Finished Size
Approximately 40 x 46 inches

Materials
- Plymouth Encore Colorspun worsted weight 75 percent acrylic/25 percent wool yarn (200 yds/100g per skein): 6 skeins pastels #7117
- Size 8 (5mm) needles or size needed to obtain gauge
- Tapestry needle

Gauge
18 sts and 24 rows = 4 inches/ 10cm in pat

To save time, take time to check gauge.

Afghan
Cast on 168 sts.

Border

Row 1 (WS): *K1, p1, rep from * across.

Row 2: *P1, k1, rep from * across.

Rows 3–5: Rep Rows 1 and 2, ending with Row 1.

Beg pat

Row 1 (RS): [P1, k1] twice, *k37, [k1, p1] twice, k37, [p1, k1] twice, rep from * once.

Row 2: [K1, p1] twice, *p37, [p1, k1] twice, p37, [k1, p1] twice, rep from * once.

Row 3: [P1, k1] twice, *k2, [yo, p1, p3tog, p1, yo, k2] 5 times, [k1, p1] twice, k2, [yo, p1, p3tog, p1, yo, k2] 5 times, [p1, k1] twice, rep from * once.

Row 4: Rep Row 2.

Rows 5–260: [Rep pat Rows 1–4] 64 times.

Border

Work 5 rows, beg and ending with border Row 2. Bind off all sts in pat.

Block lightly. ◆

Soft-as-a-Cloud Baby Afghan

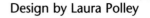

Design by Laura Polley

Knit up a reversible afghan that is full of texture and warmth. It's just the right size for cuddling your precious little one.

Skill Level
Beginner*

Finished Size
Approximately 34 by 41 inches (blocked)

Materials
- Plymouth Encore worsted weight 75 percent acrylic/25 percent wool yarn* (200 yds/100g per ball): 8 balls yellow #215
- Size 11 (8mm) 29-inch circular needle, or size needed to obtain gauge
- Tapestry needle

Gauge
12 sts and 18 rows = 4 inches/10cm in pat with 2 strands of yarn held tog

To save time, take time to check gauge.

Pattern Notes
Afghan is worked using 2 strands of yarn held tog throughout.

Circular needle is used to accommodate large number of sts; do not join but turn and work in rows.

Pattern Stitch
(multiple of 20 sts)

Row 1 (RS): *P1, k9, p9, k1, rep from * across.

Row 2: *P2, k8, p8, k2, rep from * across.

Row 3: *P3, k7, p7, k3, rep from * across.

Row 4: *P4, k6, p6, k4, rep from * across.

Row 5: *P5, k5, rep from * across.

Row 6: *P6, k4, p4, k6, rep from * across.

Row 7: *P7, k3, p3, k7, rep from * across.

Row 8: *P8, k2, p2, k8, rep from * across.

Row 9: *P9, k1, p1, k9, rep from * across.

Row 10: *P10, k10, rep from * across.

Row 11: *K10, p10, rep from * across.

Row 12: *K9, p1, k1, p9, rep from * across.

Row 13: *K8, p2, k2, p8, rep from * across.

Row 14: *K7, p3, k3, p7, rep from * across.

Row 15: *K6, p4, k4, p6, rep from * across.

Row 16: *K5, p5, rep from * across.

Row 17: *K4, p6, k6, p4, rep from * across.

Row 18: *K3, p7, k7, p3, rep from * across.

Row 19: *K2, p8, k8, p2, rep from * across.

Row 20: *K1, p9, k9, p1, rep from * across.

Row 21: Rep Row 10.

Row 22: Rep Row 11.

Rep Rows 1–22 for pat.

Afghan
With 2 strands of yarn held tog throughout, cast on 106 sts. Knit 6 rows.

Beg pat

Row 1: K3, [rep Row 1 of pat] 5 times, k3.

Row 2: K3, [rep Row 2 of pat] 5 times, k3.

Rows 3–198: Continue in established pat, keeping first and last 3 sts in garter st and center 100 sts in pat, working Rows 1–22 of pat a total of 9 times. Piece should measure approximately 40 inches from beg (slightly stretched).

Knit 6 rows. Bind off all sts.

Finishing
Block to size. ◆

Spencer the Elephant Baby

Design by Kathleen Brklacich Sasser

Put a little whimsy in your nursery with Spencer the Elephant! He's cute, he's cuddly and he will quickly become any child's best friend.

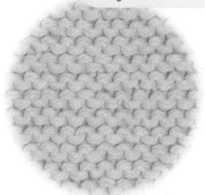

Skill Level
Advanced****

Finished Size
Approximately 33 x 45 inches

Materials
- Plymouth Encore worsted weight 75 percent acrylic/25 percent wool yarn (200 yds/100g per ball): 14 balls pink #029, 2 balls each white #208, gray #389
- Size 10 (6mm) 36-inch circular needle or size needed to obtain gauge
- Size H/8 (5mm) crochet hook
- Basting thread
- Tapestry needle

Gauge
13 sts and 18 rows = 4 inches/10cm in St st with 2 strands of yarn

To save time, take time to check gauge.

Pattern Notes
Circular needle is used to accomodate large number of sts. Do not join, work back and forth in rows.

Afghan is knitted with 2 strands of yarn held tog throughout. White portion of eyes is worked using intarsia technique; remaining details are added later with duplicate st.

Special Abbreviations
Byf: Bring yarn forward between tips of needles.

M1 (Make1): Inc by making a backward loop over right needle.

Body
With 2 strands of pink, cast on 107 sts. Work even in St st for 148 rows. Referring to Chart A, beg eyes with white on Row 149, using a separate length of yarn for each eye. Beg on Row 172, dec for shoulders following chart.

Duplicate st outlines for eyes, toes and head with 2 strands of gray.

Using 2 strands of yarn, work 2 rnds of single crochet around entire afghan with pink, followed by 1 rnd of gray. Block well.

Trunk
With 2 strands of pink, cast on 20 sts.

Rows 1–20: Knit.

Row 21: Knit, inc 1 st at each end. (22 sts)

Rows 22–26: Knit.

Row 27: Knit, inc 1 st at each end. (24 sts)

Row 28: K19, byf, sl 1 purlwise, turn.

Row 29: K15, byf, sl 1 purlwise, turn.

Row 30: K10, byf, sl 1 purlwise, turn.

Row 31: K5, byf, sl 1 purlwise, turn.

Row 32: Knit to end.

Row 33: Knit, inc 1 st at each end. (26 sts)

Rows 34–38: Knit.

Row 39: Knit, inc 1 st at each end. (28 sts)

Rows 40–46: Knit.

Row 47: Knit, inc 1 st at each end. (30 sts)

Rows 48–54: Knit.

Row 55: Knit, inc 1 st at each end. (32 sts)

Rows 56–70: Knit.

Row 71: Knit, inc 1 st at each end. (34 sts)

Rows 72–86: Knit.

Row 87: Knit, inc 1 st at each end. (36 sts)

Rows 88–102: Knit.

Row 103: Knit, inc 1 st at each end. (38 sts)

Row 104: K1, M1, k2, M1, k3, M1, k7, [k2tog] 6 times, k7, M1, k3, M1, k2, M1, k1.

Row 105: Knit, inc 1 st at each end. (40 sts)

Rows 106–110: Knit.

Row 111: K1, M1, k17, [k2tog] twice, k17, M1, k1.

Row 112: Knit, inc 1 st at each end. (42 sts)

Rows 113–115: Knit.

Rows 116–118: Knit, inc 1 st at each end. (48 sts)

Row 119: Knit.

Row 120: Knit, inc 1 st at each end. (50 sts)

Rows 121–123: Knit.

Row 124: Knit, inc 1 st at each end. (52 sts)

Rows 125–129: Knit.

Row 130: Knit, inc 1 st at each end. (54 sts)

Rows 131–139: Knit.

Bind off all sts loosely.

Seam trunk. At tip, making sure top of trunk is centered over seam line, secure with a couple of sts in center. This will prevent small hands from playing inside the trunk and will also

create a nose!

With 2 strands of gray, single crochet once around tip of trunk.

Attach trunk

Fold top of trunk in half and measure opening. Referring to photo, select desired location on face just below eyes and place a safety pin. Measure down length of trunk opening and place another safety pin. Find midpoint between these 2 safety pins, and place another pin. Now, measure sideways in same manner, placing safety pins on either side of center pin. With a contrasting basting thread, baste a circle on afghan, using 4 safety pins as reference points.

Divide top of trunk into 4 even sections beg with seam line. These four points should match 4 safety pins marked on afghan. Be sure seam line of trunk is facing afghan, then secure trunk to afghan temporarily with these pins. Sew trunk on with a whipstitch. When sewing is complete, remove all safety pins.

Ears

Make 2 alike

Note: Because garter st is reversible, there's no need to reverse shaping.

With 2 strands of pink, cast on 25 sts.

Row 1: Knit.

Row 2: K1, M1, knit to end, cast on 3 sts. (pm after 3 cast on sts to indicate bottom of ear)

Row 3: K to last st, M1, k1. (30 sts)

Row 4: K1, M1, knit to end, cast on 3 sts. (34 sts)

Row 5: K to last st, M1, k1.

Rows 6–9: Rep Rows 4 and 5. (45 sts)

Row 10: Knit to end, cast on 3. (48 sts)

Row 11: Knit to last st, M1, k1. (49 sts)

Row 12: Rep Row 10. (52 sts)

Row 13: Knit.

Row 14: Rep Row 10. (55 sts)

Row 15: Knit.

Row 16: Rep Row 11. (56 sts)

Row 17: K1, M1, knit to last st, M1, k1. (58 sts)

Row 18: Rep Row 11. (59 sts)

Row 19: Knit.

Row 20: Rep Row 11. (60 sts)

Row 21: Knit.

Row 22: Rep Row 11. (61 sts)

Row 23: K1, M1, knit to end. (62 sts)

Row 24: Knit.

Row 25: Rep Row 23. (63 sts)

Row 26–55: Knit.

Row 56: Knit to last 2 sts, k2tog. (62 sts)

Row 57: Knit.

Row 58: Rep Row 56. (61 sts)

Row 59: Knit.

Rows 60–62: Knit, dec 1 st at each end. (55 sts)

Row 63: Knit.

Row 64: Knit to last 2 sts, k2tog. (54 sts)

Row 65: Knit.

Row 66: Knit, dec 1 st at each end. (52 sts)

Rows 67–74: [Rep Rows 63–66] twice. (46 sts)

Row 75: Knit.

Row 76: Rep Row 66.

Row 77: Knit.

Rows 78–81: [Rep Rows 76 and 77] twice. (40 sts)

Row 82: Rep Row 66. (38 sts)

Row 83: K2tog, k to end. (37 sts)

Row 84: Knit, dec 1 st at each end. (35 sts)

Row 85–94: Rep Rows 83 and 84. (20 sts)

Rows 95–97: Rep Row 84. (14 sts)

Bind off all sts loosely. With 2 strands of gray and RS facing, work 1 rnd of single crochet around each ear. Be sure to flip 1 ear, in order to have a right and a left.

Attach ears

Align cast-on edge of ear over duplicate st on side of face. Sew in place. Rep for other ear. Spread ears and afghan out evenly and tack ears in place along outside edge of afghan. ◆

COLOR KEY
■ Pink
□ White
▣ Gray duplicate stitch

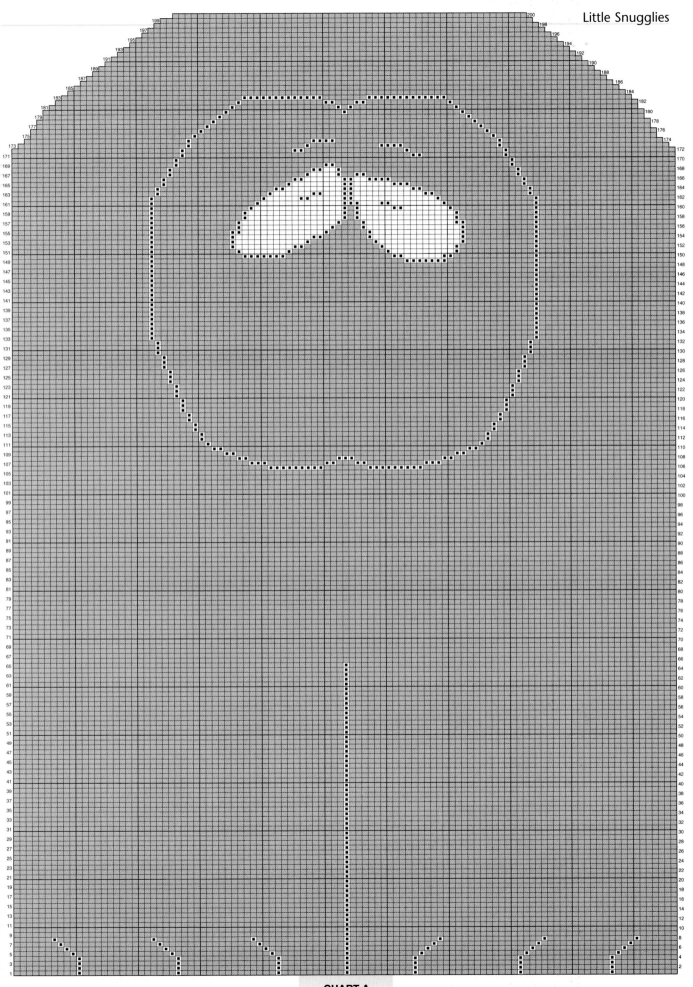

Little Snugglies

CHART A

Easy Shells Baby Blanket

Design by Ann E. Smith

This lovely blanket has the feel of elegance, but is a quick-to-knit project. The blanket is worked with two strands of yarn held together throughout.

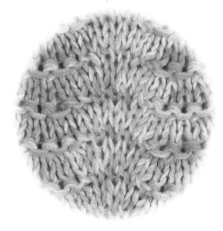

Special Abbreviation

M1 (Make 1): Lift horizontal bar lying between last st worked and next st and knit into back of it.

Pattern Stitch

Shells Pat (multiple of 11 sts + 6)

Row 1 (RS): Knit.

Row 2: K3, p across to last 3 sts, k3.

Row 3: K3, [p2tog] twice, [M1, k1] 3 times, M1, *[p2tog] 4 times, [M1, k1] 3 times, M1, rep from * across to last 7 sts, [p2tog] twice, k3.

Row 4: Rep Row 2.

Rep Rows 1–4 for pat.

Pattern Notes

Blanket is worked with 2 strands of yarn held tog throughout.

Circular needle is used to accomodate large number of sts. Do not join; turn and work in rows.

Skill Level

Beginner*

Finished Size

Approximately 35 x 45 inches

Materials

- Plymouth Encore worsted weight 75 percent acrylic/25 percent wool yarn (200 yds/100g per ball): 4 balls baby blue #793
- Plymouth Encore worsted weight Colorspun 75 percent acrylic/25 percent wool yarn (200 yds/100g per ball): 5 skeins blue/yellow/white variegated #7116
- Size 11 (8mm) circular needle or size needed to obtain gauge
- Tapestry needle

Gauge

12½ sts and 17 rows = 4 inches/ 10cm in pat with 2 strands of yarn

2 pat reps (22 sts) = 7 inches

To save time, take time to check gauge.

Blanket

Beg at lower edge with 1 strand of each color, cast on 105 sts. Rep pat Rows 1–4 until piece measures approximately 45 inches from beg, ending with Row 4.

Knit 1 row. Bind off all sts loosely and knitwise on WS. ◆

Busy Blanket

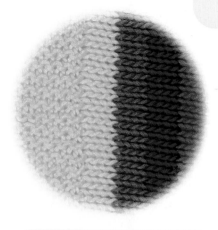

Design by Diane Zangl

Let the baby games begin on this playpad for the young set. Different shaped pockets at each corner hide toys and treasures to keep baby entertained.

Skill Level
Easy**

Finished Size
Approximately 45 x 45 inches (blocked)

Materials
- Plymouth Wildflower DK weight 51 percent cotton/49 percent acrylic yarn (136 yds/50g per ball): 12 balls yellow #48 (MC), 3 balls each jungle green #49 and royal blue #57, 2 balls red #46
- Size 5 (3.75mm) needles or size needed to obtain gauge
- 1 (1¼-inch) button
- Tapestry needle

Gauge
20 sts and 20 rows = 4 inches/10cm in garter st

20 sts and 30 rows = 4 inches/10cm in St st

To save time, take time to check gauge.

Special Abbreviations
M1L (Make 1 Left): Make a clockwise loop and place on RH needle.

M1R (Make 1 Right): Make a counterclockwise loop and place on RH needle.

Pattern Stitches
Border Pat

Row 1 (RS): K1, M1L, k to last st, M1R, k1.

Row 2: Purl.

Rep Rows 1 and 2 for pat.

Color Sequence

Work 4 rows each of yellow, green, blue, red.

Center
With MC, cast on 165 sts. Work even in garter st until there are 165 ridges. (330 rows)

Bind off all sts.

Border
With RS facing and MC, pick up and k 1 st in each st along cast-on edge.

Work in border pat and color sequence until there are 44 rows. (11 stripes)

Change to MC and work in garter st for 5 rows. Bind off on WS.

Rep border along bound-off edge.

For end borders, pick up and k 1 st in each ridge. Rep border.

Pockets
Pocket #1

With MC, cast on 30 sts. Work even in garter st until pocket measures 6 inches. Bind off all sts.

Pocket #2

Make 1 red, 1 blue

Cast on 30 sts. Work even in garter st until pocket measures 3 inches. Bind off all sts.

Pocket #3

With green, cast on 30 sts. Work even in garter st until pocket measures 5½ inches. Bind off all sts.

Pocket flap

With MC, cast on 31 sts. Work in garter st, dec 1 st each end every other row until 3 sts remain.

Work I-cord on these 3 sts for 2 inches. K last 3 sts tog and fasten off.

Cut yarn leaving an 8-inch strand. Sew end of I-cord to point of flap for button loop.

Pocket #4

Make 1 red, 1 blue

Cast on 31 sts. Work as for pocket flap until 3 sts remain. Bind off all sts.

Finishing
Sew corner seams of border.

Referring to photo for placement, sew one pocket to each corner. Sew button under loop of pocket flap. Block. ◆

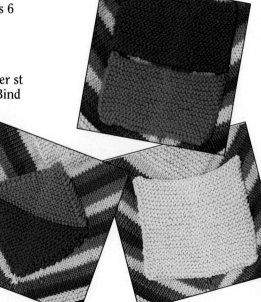

Tilt-a-Whirl Baby Afghan

Design by Jill Wolcott

Could modular knitting be more fun? Knit each block separately from the center out and join as you go or save the joining for the end.

Skill Level
Advanced****

Finished Measurements
Afghan: Approximately 32 x 40 inches

Individual squares: 8 inches

Materials
- Plymouth Encore worsted weight 75 percent acrylic/25 percent wool yarn (200 yds/100g per ball): 3 balls each red #1386, green #054, blue #133, yellow #1382
- Size 8 (5mm) set of 5 double-pointed and 24-inch circular needles or size needed to obtain gauge
- Waste yarn or stitch holders
- Stitch markers (optional)
- Tapestry needle

Gauge
15 sts and 47 rows = 4 inches/10cm in pat (blocked)

16 sts and 42 rows = 4 inches/10cm in pat (unblocked)

To save time, take time to check gauge.

Special Abbreviations
CS#: Color sequence number

K1below: K into top of st below first st on needle, then k st on needle. (inc 1)

P1below: P into top of st below first st on needle, then p st on needle. (inc 1)

3 bdl bind off: With sts from both sides

on needles and RS tog, hold needles tog and parallel in left hand. With dpn and color of yarn last knitted, k first st from each needle tog, *k next st on both needles tog and bind off 1 st, rep from * to end, cut yarn and draw through last st.

Pattern Notes
Color Sequences:

#1: Green (A), blue (B), yellow (C), red (D)

#2: Blue (A), red (B), green (C), yellow (D)

#3: Yellow (A), green (B), red (C), blue (D)

#4: Red (A), yellow (B), blue (C), green (D)

Finishing Methods: You may join squares as you go (see page 88), or knit all 24 squares and join them later (see page 89).

To join as you go, follow sequence given in chart and written instructions. Each square is made separately, then joined. For specific directions see Assembling as You Go (see page 88).

If you prefer to knit all squares before joining, you will need a total of 6 squares in each color sequence, 3 in each pat sequence. For specific directions see Assembling at the End (see page 89).

Row 1	4 1 Block I 3 CS#1 2	4 1 Block II 3 CS#4 2	4 1 Block I 3 CS#2 2	4 1 Block II 3 CS#3 2
Row 2	4 1 Block II 3 CS#2 2	4 1 Block I 3 CS#3 2	4 1 Block II 3 CS#1 2	4 1 Block I 3 CS#4 2
Row 3	4 1 Block I 3 CS#4 2	4 1 Block II 3 CS#1 2	4 1 Block I 3 CS#3 2	4 1 Block II 3 CS#2 2
Row 4	4 1 Block II 3 CS#2 2	4 1 Block I 3 CS#3 2	4 1 Block II 3 CS#4 2	4 1 Block I 3 CS#1 2
Row 5	4 1 Block I 3 CS#1 2	4 1 Block II 3 CS#4 2	4 1 Block I 3 CS#2 2	4 1 Block II 3 CS#3 2
Row 6	4 1 Block II 3 CS#3 2	4 1 Block I 3 CS#2 2	4 1 Block II 3 CS#1 2	4 1 Block I 3 CS#4 2

FIG. 1

Rnd 18)

Change to D.

Rnd 19: Knit. (44 sts)

Rnds 20, 22 and 24: *P1below, p remaining sts on needle, rep from * around. (14 sts on each needle after Rnd 24)

Rnds 21 and 23: Purl. Change to A.

Rnds 25, 27 and 29: Knit.

Rnds 26 and 28: *K1below, k remaining sts on needle, rep from * around. (16 sts on each needle after Rnd 28)

Rnd 30: *[K1below] twice, k remaining sts on needle, rep from * around. (18 sts on each needle)

Change to B.

Rnd 31: Knit.

Rnds 32 and 34: *P1below, p remaining sts on needle, rep from * around. (20 sts on each needle after Rnd 34)

Rnds 33 and 35: Purl.

Rnd 36: *[P1below] twice, p remaining sts on needle, rep from * around. (22 sts on each needle)

Change to C.

Note: At this point, you may want to switch to a 24-inch circular needle, marking each section with a ring marker and using a different color to indicate beg of rnd.

Rnds 37, 39 and 31: Knit.

Rnds 38 and 40: *K1below, k remaining sts on needle, rep from * around. (24 sts in each section after Rnd 40)

Rnd 42: *[K1below] twice, k remaining sts on needle, rep from * around. (26 sts in each section)

Change to D.

Rnd 43: Knit.

Rnds 44 and 46: *P1below, p remaining sts on needle, rep from * around. (28 sts in each section after Rnd 46)

Rnds 45 and 47: Purl.

Rnd 48: *[P1below] twice, p remaining sts on needle, rep from * around. (30 sts in ea section)

Weave in ends, working from center out.

Block II

With A, cast on 8 sts. Divide sts evenly on 4 needles, then join without twisting. Mark beg of rnd.

Block I

With A, cast on 8 sts. Divide sts evenly on 4 needles, then join without twisting. Mark beg of rnd.

Rnds 1, 3 and 5: Knit.

Rnds 2, 4 and 6: *K1below, k rem sts on needle, rep from * around. (5 sts on each needle after Rnd 6)

Change to B.

Rnd 7: Knit. (20 sts)

Rnds 8, 10 and 12: *P1below, p remaining sts on needle, rep from * around. (8 sts on each needle after Rnd 12)

Rnds 9 and 11: Purl. Change to C.

Rnds 13, 15 and 17: Knit.

Rnds 14, 16 and 18: *K1below, k remaining sts on needle, rep from * around. (11 sts on each needle after

Continued on page 87

Baby Animal Sampler

Design by Bonnie Lively

This colorful afghan is worked from a color chart in a combination of Fair Isle and intarsia. The cute animals and flowers will charm any toddler.

Pattern Stitch

Seed St (odd number of sts)

Row 1: K1, *p1, k1, rep from * across.

Rep Row 1 for pat.

Front

With MC, cast on 149 sts and work 12 rows of seed st. On last row, pm 6 sts in from each edge.

Beg pat

Keeping 6 sts at each edge in MC and established seed st throughout, beg with a RS row, work pat from Chart A across center 137 sts, using markers to separate panels if desired. At end of chart, remove markers, work 12 more rows of seed st with MC. Bind off all sts in pat.

Back

With MC, cast on 135 sts and work in St st until piece measures 34 inches. Bind off all sts.

Finishing

Block pieces and sew side and end seams.

Skill Level

Advanced****

Finished Size

Approximately 27 x 34 inches

Materials

- Plymouth Encore DK weight 75 percent acrylic/25 percent wool yarn (150 yds/50g per ball): 6 balls Colorspun Tweed (#7357) variegated pastels (MC), 2 balls each red #9601, gold #1014, 1 skein each off-white #146, soft yellow #215, burgundy #999, purple #1384, blue #133, green #054
- Size 6 (4mm) needles or size needed to obtain gauge
- Stitch markers
- Tapestry needle

Gauge

23 sts and 32 rows = 4 inches/10cm in St st and color pat

20 sts and 26 rows = 4 inches/10cm in plain St st (back)

To save time, take time to check gauge.

Embellishment

Referring to photo, be creative in adding texture and embroidery to different panels. Designer used MC and French knots in centers of flowers to tack front and back pieces.

Embroider flowers in long burgundy stripe using back st and running st. Clouds and birds in sunset panel are worked in back st. ◆

**CHART A
TOP LEFT**

*Note: Rows 2, 8, 20, 208, 220 and 226
are knit on WS, forming a garter st ridge.*

COLOR KEY

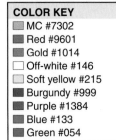

- MC #7302
- Red #9601
- Gold #1014
- Off-white #146
- Soft yellow #215
- Burgundy #999
- Purple #1384
- Blue #133
- Green #054

**CHART A
TOP RIGHT**

Tilt-a-Whirl continued from page 83

Rnds 1, 3 and 5: Purl.

Rnds 2, 4 and 6: *P1below, p remaining sts on needle, rep from * around. (5 sts on each needle after Rnd 6)

Change to B.

Rnds 7, 9 and 11: Knit. (20 sts)

Rnds 8, 10 and 12: *K1below, k remaining sts on needle, rep from * around. (8 sts on each needle after Rnd 12)

Change to C.

Rnd 13: Knit.

Rnds 14, 16 and 18: *P1below, p remaining sts on needle, rep from * around. (11 sts on each needle after Rnd 18)

Rnds 15 and 17: Purl. Change to D.

Rnds 19, 21 and 23: Knit. (44 sts)

Rnds 20, 22 and 24: *K1below, k remaining sts on needle, rep from * around. (14 sts on each needle after Rnd 24)

Change to A.

Rnd 25: Knit.

Rnds 26 and 28: *P1below, p remaining sts on needle, rep from * around. (16 sts on each needle after Rnd 28)

Rnds 27 and 29: Purl.

Rnd 30: *[P1below] twice, p remaining sts on needle, rep from * around. (18 sts on each needle)

Change to B.

Rnds 31, 33 and 35: Knit.

Rnds 32 and 34: *K1below, k remaining sts on needle, rep from * around. (20 sts on each needle after Rnd 34)

Rnd 36: *[K1below] twice, k remaining sts on needle, rep from * around. (22 sts on each needle)

Change to C.

Note: At this point, you may want to switch to a 24-inch circular needle, marking each section with a ring marker and using a different color to indicate beg of rnd.

Rnd 37: Knit.

**CHART A
BOTTOM LEFT**

Note: *Rows 2, 8, 20, 208, 220 and 226 are knit on WS, forming a garter st ridge.*

Tilt-a-Whirl Baby Aghan

Rnds 38 and 40: *P1below, p remaining sts on needle, rep from * around. (24 sts in each section)

Rnds 39 and 41: Purl.

Rnd 42: *[P1below] twice, p remaining sts on needle, rep from * around. (26 sts in each section)

Change to D.

Rnds 43, 45 and 47: Knit.

Rnds 44 and 46: *K1below, k remaining sts on needle, rep from * around. (28 sts in each section)

Rnd 48: *[K1below] twice, k remaining sts on needle, rep from * around. (30 sts in each section)

Weave in ends, working from center out.

Assembling as You Go

Referring to Fig.1 (see page 82), beg in upper

**CHART A
BOTTOM RIGHT**

Return side 3 of previous square to needle and join to side 1 with 3 ndl bind off, using last color of this square. Place sides 2 and 3 on holders. Return side 2 of Square 2, Row 1 to needle and join to side 4 with 3 ndl bind off, using last color of this square. Cut yarn and weave end in, joining to previous squares and closing gap. Make a Block II/CS# 1 square. Rep joining above, joining to previous square and corresponding square in row above. Make a Block I/CS# 4 square. Rep joining above, placing only side 2 on holder and bind off side 3.

Afghan Row 3: Follow joining directions for Row 2. Make a Block I/CS#4 square, a Block II/CS#1 square, a Block I/CS#3 square, and a Block II/CS#2 square.

Afghan Row 4: Follow joining directions for Row 2. Make a Block II/CS#2 square, a Block I/CS#3 square, a Block II/CS#4 square, and a Block I/CS#1 square.

Afghan Row 5: Follow joining directions for Row 2. Make a Block I/CS#1 square, a Block II/CS#4 square, a Block I/CS#2 square, and a Block II/CS#3 square.

Afghan Row 6: Make a Block II/CS#3 square. Bind off sides 1 and 2. Place side 3 on holder. Return side 2 of Square 1, Row 5 to needle and join to side 4 with 3 ndl bind off, using last color of this square. Weave in ends, joining to previous row. Make a Block I/CS#2 square. Return side 3 of previous square to needle and join to side 1 with 3 ndl bind off, using last color of this square. Bind off side 2. Place side 3 on holder. Return side 2 of corresponding square in row above and join to side 4 with 3 ndl bind off, using last color of this square. Cut yarn and weave in ends, joining to previous row and square. Make a Block II/CS#1 square. Rep joining instructions above. Make a Block I/CS#4 square. Return side 3 of previous square to needle and join to side 1 with 3 ndl bind off, using last color of this square. Bind off sides 2 and 3. Return side 2 of corresponding square in row above and join to side 4 with 3 ndl bind off, using last color of this square. Cut yarn and weave in ends, joining to previous row and square.

Assembling at the End

Work all 24 squares, placing each edge on a separate holder or piece of waste yarn.

Referring to Fig. 1 (see page 82) and Assembling as You Go instructions, put squares tog, using ends to close gaps where 4 squares meet. ◆

left corner and work across row to right. Subsequent rows are worked from left to right. When binding off for edges, Bind off all sts loosely and knitwise. Place each remaining side on a separate holder or piece of waste yarn as indicated.

Afghan Row 1: Make a Block I/CS#1 square. Bind off side 1. Place sides 2 and 3 on holders. Join yarn and bind off side 4. Make a Block II/CS#4 square. *Return side 3 of previous square to needles and join to side 1 with 3 needle bind off, using last color of this square. Place sides 2 and 3 on holders. Join yarn and bind off side 4. Cut yarn and

join to previous square. Make a Block I/CS#2 square. Rep joining instructions from * above. Make a Block II/CS#3 square. Return side 3 of previous square to needles and join to side 1 with 3 ndl bind off, using last color of this square. Place side 2 on holder. Join yarn and bind off sides 3 and 4. Cut yarn and join to previous square.

Afghan Row 2: Make a Block II/CS#2 square. Bind off side 1. Place sides 2 and 3 on holders. Return side 2 of Square 1, Row 1 to needle and join to side 4 with 3 ndl bind off, using last color of this square. Make a Block I/CS#3 square.

Christmas at Home

*Y*ou'll find many uses for this collection of festive Christmas afghans throughout the holiday season, from covering your little ones as they wait for Santa to snuggling with your sweetie after a night of wrapping gifts.

Chapter 5

Candlelight Christmas Afghan

Design by Frances Hughes

Enjoy the romance of the Christmas season snuggled under this lovely afghan. It's easy to knit and fun to use. Knit it for Christmas or in colors to match your sofa.

Skill Level
Easy**

Finished Size
Approximately 46 x 60 inches

Materials
- Plymouth Encore worsted weight 75 percent acrylic/25 percent wool yarn (200 yds/100g per ball): 3 balls gold #1014, 4 balls each green #054, red #9601
- Size 8 (5mm) 29-inch circular needle or size needed to obtain gauge
- Size 9 (5.5mm) 29-inch circular needle
- Size 10 (6mm) 29-inch circular needle
- Cable needle
- Tapestry needle

Gauge
16 sts = 4 inches/10cm in garter st with smallest needle

To save time, take time to check gauge.

Special Abbreviations
M3 (Make 3): [K1, p1, k1] in next st.

C6 (Cluster 6): K2, p2, k2, sl 6 sts just worked to cn, wrap yarn counterclockwise around sts twice, then sl them back to RH needle.

Afghan
With size 8 needle and A, cast on 180 sts.

Pattern 1
Rows 1–38: With A, knit. (end of Pat 1)

With B, knit 2 rows, with A, knit 2 rows.

Pattern 2
Work with size 9 needle and B.

Rows 1 and 2: Knit.

Row 3: K5, p to last 5 sts, end k5.

Row 4: K6, *M3, p3tog, rep from * to last 6 sts, end k6.

Row 5: Knit.

Row 6: K6, *p3tog, M3, rep from * to last 6 sts, end k6.

Rows 7–50: [Rep Rows 3–6] 11 times.

Rows 51 and 52: Knit. (end of Pat 2)

With C, knit 2 rows; with B, knit 2 rows.

Pattern 3
Work with size 10 needle and C.

Row 1: K5, p2, *k2, p2, rep from * across to last 5 sts, end k5.

Row 2: K7, *p2, k2, rep from * across to last 5 sts, end k5.

Row 3: K5, p2, *C6, p2, rep from * across to last 5 sts, end k5.

Row 4: Rep Row 2.

Row 5: Rep Row 1.

Row 6: Rep Row 2.

Row 7: K5, p2, k2, p2, *C6, p2, rep from * across to last 9 sts, end k2, p2, k5.

Row 8: Rep Row 2.

Rows 9–120: [Rep Rows 1–8] 14 times more. (end of Pat 3)

With B, knit 2 rows; with C, knit 2 rows.

Pattern 4
With size 9 needle and B, rep Rows 1–52 of Pat 2.

With A, knit 2 rows; with B, knit 2 rows.

Pattern 5
With size 8 needle and A, rep Rows 1–38 of Pat 1.

Bind off all sts and block to shape. ◆

Candy Cane Afghan

Design by Dixie L. Butler

Quick to knit and reversible, this afghan is great for any holiday. Just change the colors to suit the occasion or select colors to match your home.

Skill Level
Beginner*

Finished Size
Approximately 44 x 64 inches

Materials
- Plymouth Encore Chunky bulky weight 75 percent acrylic/25 percent wool yarn (143 yds/100g per ball): 14 balls white #208 (MC), 5 balls red #1386 (CC)
- Size 15 (10mm) circular needle or size needed to obtain gauge
- Tapestry needle

Gauge
8 sts and 12 rows = 4 inches/10cm in pat with 2 strands of yarn held tog

To save time, take time to check gauge.

Pattern Notes
Circular needle is used to accomodate large number of sts. Do not join at end of row.

Afghan is knitted with 2 strands of yarn held tog throughout. Color A is 2 strands of MC; color B is 1 strand of MC and 1 strand of CC.

Afghan
With A, cast on 109 sts.

Row 1: *K3, p1, rep from * across, ending k1.

Rep Row 1 for pat until piece measures 10 inches, cut 1 strand of MC, join 1 strand of CC (color B) and work until color B stripe measures 8 inches. Rep these 2 stripes until piece measures approximately 64 inches, ending with color A. There will be 4 stripes of A and 3 stripes of B.

Bind off all sts. ◆

Kente Afghan for Kwaanza

Design by Uyvonne Bigham

Celebrate Kwanza with this striking afghan featuring a Fair Isle design with a black garter stitch border and center.

Skill Level

Intermediate***

Finished Size

Approximately 45 x 60 inches

Materials

- Plymouth Encore worsted weight 75 percent acrylic/25 percent wool yarn (200 yds/100g per ball): 8 balls black #217 (MC), 1 ball each white #208, green #054, orange #1383, blue #133, burgundy #999
- Size 8 (5mm) needles
- Size 9 (5.5mm) needles or size needed to obtain gauge
- 2 stitch holders
- Tapestry needle

Gauge

20 sts = 4 inches/10cm in St st and color pat with larger needles

To save time, take time to check gauge.

Bottom Border

With smaller needles and MC, cast on 201 sts and work 4 rows garter st. Change to larger needles and beg color pat, keeping 4 MC sts at each edge in garter st throughout.

Row 1 (RS): K4 MC; work color pat from Chart A to last 4 sts; k4 MC.

Rows 2–24: Work in established color pat,

Continued on page 110

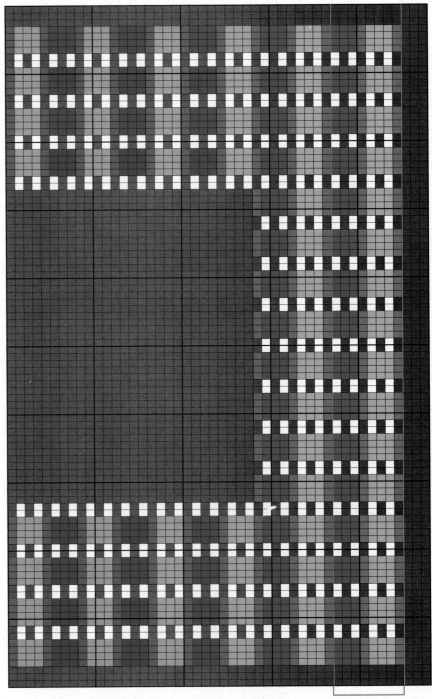

COLOR KEY
- ■ Black (MC)
- ■ Orange
- ■ Blue
- ■ Burgundy
- □ White
- ■ Green

FIG. 1

Rep

Note: Only right end of afghan is shown.

CHAPTER 5

Christmas Forest Afghan

Design by JoAnne Turcotte

This clever afghan uses a novel construction technique similar to a finely pieced quilt to create strips of mitered squares.

Skill Level
Intermediate***

Finished Size
Approximately 51 x 59 inches

Materials
- Plymouth Encore Chunky bulky weight 75 percent acrylic/25 percent wool yarn (143 yds/100g per ball): 6 balls red #1386, 5 balls each Aran #256 and dark green #204
- Size 9 (5.5mm) 24-inch or longer circular needle
- Size 10 (6mm) needles or size needed to obtain gauge
- Tapestry needle

Gauge
12 sts = 4 inches/10cm in pat with larger needles (Each mitered square should measure approximately 5½ inches square)

To save time, take time to check gauge.

Special Abbreviation
Cdd (Central double decrease): Sl next 2 sts as if to k2tog, k1, p2sso.

Beg with red, cast on 41 sts. Knit 1 row.

Basic Mitered Square Pattern
Row 1 (RS): K19, cdd, k19.

Row 2: Purl.

Row 3: K18, cdd, k18.

Row 4: K to center st (k18), p center st, k to end of row.

Row 5: K17, cdd, k17.

Row 6: Purl.

Row 7: K16, cdd, k16.

Row 8: K to center st, p1, k to end of row.

Continue established dec in Rows 5–8, purling center st on all WS rows until 3 sts remain, ending with a WS row.

Last row: Work cdd.

Pull yarn through remaining st. Cut

72 C	70 C	67 C	63 C	58 C	52 C	45 C	37 A
71 C	68 C	64 C	59 C	53 C	46 C	38 C	29 A
69 C	65 C	60 C	54 C	47 C	39 C	30 C	22 A
66 C	61 C	55 C	48 C	40 C	31 C	23 C	16 A
62 C	56 C	49 C	41 C	32 C	24 C	17 C	11 A
57 C	50 C	42 C	33 C	25 C	18 C	12 C	7 A
51 C	43 C	34 C	26 C	19 C	13 C	8 C	4 A
44 C	35 C	27 C	20 C	14 C	9 C	5 C	2 A
36 B	28 B	21 B	15 B	10 B	6 B	3 B	1 A

FIG. 1

Note: Squares are worked in color and sequence as numbered, following instructions for Square A, B or C as indicated.

Continued on page 111

Blue Christmas Afghan

Design by Lynnette Harter

This bulky reversible afghan is perfect for the beginning knitter and looks great in any color.

Pattern Note

Circular needle is used to accomodate large number of sts. Do not join at end of row.

Afghan

Cast on 120 sts.

Rows 1–4: *K4, p4, rep from * across.

Rows 5 and 7: P2, *k4, p4, rep from * across, end p2.

Rows 6 and 8: K2, *p4, k4, rep from * across, end k2.

Rows 9–12: *P4, k4, rep from * across.

Rows 13 and 15: Rep Row 6.

Rows 14 and 16: Rep Row 5.

Rep Rows 1–16 for pat until afghan measures approximately 60 inches from beg, ending with Row 4, 8, 12 or 16. Bind off all sts.

Skill Level

Beginner*

Finished Size

Approximately 40 x 60 inches (excluding fringe)

Materials

- Plymouth Encore Chunky bulky weight 75 percent acrylic/25 percent wool yarn (143 yds/100g per ball): 10 balls blue #515
- Size 13 (9mm) 32-inch circular needle or size needed to obtain gauge
- Tapestry needle
- Crochet hook (for fringe)

Gauge

12 sts = 4 inches/10cm in pat

To save time, take time to check gauge.

Fringe

For each fringe, *cut 2 (12-inch) strands of yarn, fold in half. Insert crochet hook through st from back to front, pull folded ends through, pull ends through loop and pull snug. Rep from * in every other st across shorter edges of afghan. Trim fringe evenly. ◆

3-D Diamonds Afghan

Design by Joyce Englund

If you crave texture and lace, this afghan will more than fill your needs. Knit yarn overs and bobbles to create the diamonds in this special afghan.

Skill Level
Intermediate***

Finished Size
Approximately 45 x 55 inches

Materials
• Plymouth Encore worsted weight 75 percent acrylic/25 percent wool yarn (200 yds/100g per ball): 13 balls dark green #1604
• Size 11 (8mm) circular needle or size needed to obtain gauge
• 2 stitch markers (optional)
• Tapestry needle

Gauge
11 sts = 4 inches/10cm in seed st with 2 strands of yarn held tog

To save time, take time to check gauge.

Pattern Notes
Afghan is worked with double strand of yarn throughout.

Circular needle is used to accomodate large number of sts. Do not join at end of row.

Special Abbreviations
Cdd (Central double decrease): Sl next 2 sts as if to k2tog, k1, p2sso.

MB (Make Bobble): [K in front, back, front, and back] of next st, pass 3 sts individually over st nearest tip of needle.

Pattern Stitches
Seed st (even number of sts)
Row 1: *K1, p1, rep from * across.
Row 2: K the purl sts, p the knit sts.
Rep Rows 1 and 2 for pat.

Diamond Pat (multiple of 16 sts + 1)
Row 1: K1, * yo, ssk, k11, k2 tog, yo, k1, rep from* across.
Row 2 and all WS rows: Purl.
Row 3: K2, *yo, ssk, k9, k2tog, yo, k3, rep from * across, end last rep k2.
Row 5: K3, *yo, ssk, k7, k2tog, yo, k5, rep from * across, end last rep k3.
Row 7: K4, *yo, ssk, k5, k2tog, yo, k7, rep from * across, end last rep k4.
Row 9: K5, *yo, ssk, k3, k2tog, yo, k4, MB, k4, rep from * across, end yo, ssk, k3, k2tog, yo, k5.
Row 11: K6, *yo, ssk, k1, k2tog, yo, k4, MB, p1, MB, k4, rep from * across, end yo, ssk, k1, k2tog, yo, k6.
Row 13: K7, *yo, cdd, yo, k4, [MB, p1] twice, MB, k4, rep from * across, end yo, cdd, yo, k7.
Row 15: K5, k2tog, *yo, k3, yo, ssk, k3, MB, p1, MB, k3, k2tog, rep from *across, end yo, k3, yo, ssk, k5.
Row 17: K4, k2tog, *yo, k5, yo, ssk, k3, MB, k3, k2tog, rep from * across, end yo, k5, yo, ssk, k4.
Row 19: K3, k2tog, *yo, k7, yo, ssk, k5, k2tog, rep from * across, end yo, k7, yo, ssk, k3.
Row 21: K2, k2tog, *yo, k4, MB, k4, yo, ssk, k3, k2tog, rep from * across, end yo, k4, MB, k4, yo, ssk, k2.
Row 23: K1, k2tog, *yo, k4, MB, p1, MB, k4, yo, ssk, k1, k2tog, rep from * across, end last rep yo, ssk, k1.
Row 25: K2tog, *yo, k4, [MB, p1] twice, MB, k4, yo, cdd, rep from *across, end last rep yo, ssk.
Row 27: K2, *yo, ssk, k3, MB, p1, MB, k3, k2tog, yo, k3, rep from * across, end last rep k2.
Row 29: K3, *yo, ssk, k3, MB, k3, k2tog, yo, k5, rep from * across, end last rep k3.
Row 31: K4, *yo, ssk, k5, k2tog, yo, k7, rep from * across, end last rep k4.
Row 32: Purl.
Rep Rows 9–32 for pat.

With double strand of yarn, cast on 125 sts. Beg with a k st, work 6 rows of seed st. On last row, pm after 6th st from each end of row.

Continuing established 6 st seed st borders on each side throughout, work diamonds pat until 9 half diamonds have been worked on each edge, omitting bobbles in last half diamonds across top of afghan. Work 6 rows of seed st.

Bind off all sts knitwise on RS. ◆

Cathedral Windows

Design by Laura Polley

A combination of fibers and an allover lace pattern turn this afghan into a fantastic beginners' project.

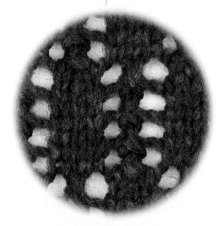

Pattern Notes

Afghan is worked with 2 strands A and 1 strand B held tog throughout.

Circular needle is used to accomodate large number of sts. Do not join at end of row.

Pattern Stitch

Cathedral Windows Pat (multiple of 6 sts + 5)

Rows 1, 3, 5 and 7 (RS): K1, *yo, sl 1, k2tog, psso, yo, k3, rep from * to last 4 sts, yo, sl 1, k2tog, psso, yo, k1.

Row 2 and all WS rows: Purl.

Rows 9, 11, 13 and 15: K4, *yo, sl 1, k2tog, psso, yo, k3, rep from * to last st, k1.

Row 16: Purl.

Rep Rows 1–16 for pat.

Afghan

With 2 strands A and 1 strand B held tog, loosely cast on 119 sts.

Work [Rows 1–16 of pat] 12 times, then rep [Rows 1–8] once. Bind off all sts loosely.

Fringe

Wrap each yarn separately around

Skill Level

Easy**

Finished Size

Approximately 50 x 58 inches (blocked, but not including fringe)

Materials

- Plymouth Encore worsted weight 75 percent acrylic/25 percent wool yarn (200 yds/100g per ball): 11 balls cranberry #1607 (A)
- Cleckheaton Mohair 12-ply worsted weight 92 percent mohair/4 percent wool/4 percent nylon yarn (110 yds/50g per ball) from Plymouth Yarns: 11 balls cranberry #267 (B)
- Size 13 (9mm) 32-inch circular needle or size needed to obtain gauge
- Size K/10½ (6.5mm) crochet hook (for fringe)
- Tapestry needle
- 8½-inch-wide piece of cardboard

Gauge

19 sts and 27½ rows = 8 inches/20cm in pat with 3 strands of yarn (blocked)

To save time, take time to check gauge.

cardboard; cut along 1 edge.

*For each fringe, take 2 strands of A and B, fold in half, forming a loop. Beg at corner, with RS of afghan facing, insert crochet hook in st from back to front, pull loop through, pull yarn ends through loop and tighten. Rep from * in every other st across upper and lower edges of afghan. Trim fringe as needed. ◆

Pine Forest Afghan

Design by E. J. Slayton

Diamond pathways enclose duplicate stitched trees in an eye-pleasing afghan. Knit in panels, this afghan is sure to become a family favorite.

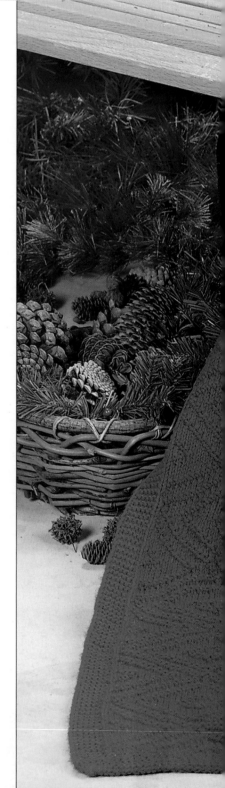

Skill Level
Advanced Beginner**

Finished Size
Approximately 42 x 48 inches

Materials
• Plymouth Encore worsted weight 75 percent acrylic/25 percent wool yarn (200 yds/100g per ball): 8 skeins red #9601, 1 ball green #054
• Size 6 (4mm) needles or size needed to obtain gauge
• Stitch markers
• Tapestry needle

Gauge
20 sts and 30 rows = 4 inches/10cm in St st

To save time, take time to check gauge.

Pattern Notes
Afghan panels are knitted with MC, then trees are duplicate stitched with CC. There will be 5 trees on each outside panel and 6 trees in center panel.

Chart does not show borders and selvage sts.

Right Panel
With MC, cast on 64 sts.

Row 1 (WS): Knit across.

Row 2: Sl 1, knit across.

Rows 3–11: Rep Rows 1 and 2, ending with Row 1.

Row 12: Sl 1, k6, pm, k to last 2 sts, pm, k2.

Row 13: K1, p1, M1, [p11, M1] 5 times, end p1, k6. (70 sts)

Beg pat

Row 1 (RS): Sl 1, k6, work Row 1 of pat from chart between markers, end k2.

Referring to chart, work [Rows 1–60 of pat] 5 times, then rep [Rows 1–31] once, sl first st every RS row and knitting first st every WS row throughout.

Next row (WS): Knit, dec 6 sts evenly across. (64 sts)

Work 9 rows of garter st, bind off knit-wise on WS.

Center Panel
With MC, cast on 59 sts.

Row 1 (WS): Knit across.

Rows 2–12: Rep Row 1, pm 2 sts in from each edge on Row 12.

Rows 3–11: Rep Rows 1 and 2, ending with Row 1.

Row 13: K1, p1, M1, [p11, M1] 5 times, end p1, k1. (65 sts)

Beg pat

Row 1 (RS): K2, work Row 31 of pat from chart between markers, end k2.

Referring to chart, work [Rows 31–60] once, then work [Rows 1–60] 5 times, rep Row 1.

Complete as for right panel. (59 sts remaining after dec row)

Left Panel
Work as for right panel, reversing border placement, sl first st of every WS row and knitting first st of every RS row.

Finishing
Sew panels tog, placing garter borders at outside edges.

With CC and tapestry needle, duplicate st trees in St st diamonds.

Chart on page 111

Christmas Ornaments Afghan

Design by Uyvonne Bigham

This afghan will be on everyone's wish list this Christmas. Bells, candles, wreaths and trees combine to give everyone a merry Christmas.

Skill Level
Easy**

Finished Size
Approximately 42 x 54 inches

Materials
- Plymouth Encore Chunky bulky weight 75 percent acrylic/25 percent wool yarn (143 yds/100g per ball): 9 balls Aran #256 (MC), 1 ball each dark green #204, dark brown #1444, red #9601, yellow #1382, black #217
- Size 10 (6mm) needles or size needed to obtain gauge
- Tapestry needle

Gauge
14 sts and 18 rows = 4 inches/ 10cm in St st

To save time, take time to check gauge.

Pattern Notes
Instructions are given for knitting afghan in 1 piece, followed by instructions for making it in strips.

Afghan is knitted with MC, then ornaments are worked in duplicate st.

Afghan in 1 Piece
With MC, cast on 130 sts.

Rows 1–8: Knit.

Row 9 (RS): Knit.

Row 10: [K4, p17] 6 times, end k4.

Rows 11–32: [Rep Rows 9 and 10] 11 times. (24 rows total)

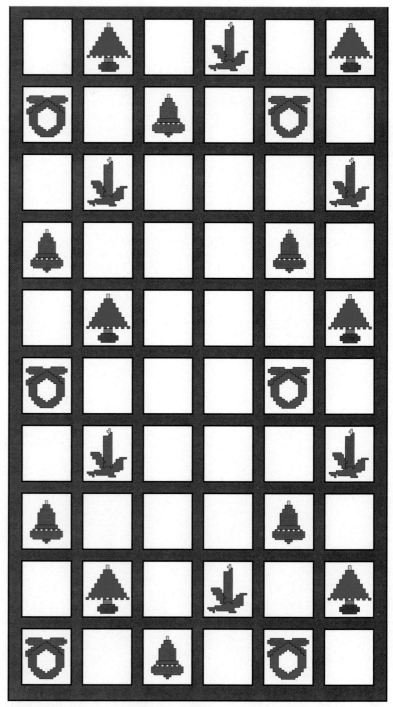

FIG. 1

Rows 33–36: Knit.

Rows 37–288: [Rep Rows 9–36] 9 times.

Rows 289–292: Knit.

Bind off all sts.

COLOR KEY
☐ Aran (MC)
■ Dark green
■ Dark brown
■ Red
☐ Yellow
■ Black

Finishing

Referring to charts and Fig. 1, duplicate st ornaments on afghan.

Afghan in Panels

Right Panel

Make 1

With MC, cast on 44 sts.

Rows 1–8: Knit.

Row 9 (RS): Knit.

Row 10: [K4, p17] twice, end k2.

Rows 11–32: [Rep Rows 9 and 10] 11 times. (24 rows total)

Rows 33–36: Knit.

Rows 37–288: [Rep Rows 9–36] 9 times.

Rows 289–292: Knit.

Bind off all sts.

Center Panel

Make 1

With MC, cast on 42 sts.

Rows 1–8: Knit.

Row 9 (RS): Knit.

Row 10: K2, p17, k4, p17, k2.

Rows 11–32: [Rep Rows 9 and 10] 11 times. (24 rows total)

Rows 33–36: Knit.

Rows 37–288: [Rep Rows 9–36] 9 times.

Rows 289–292: Knit.

Bind off all sts.

Left Panel

Make 1

With MC, cast on 44 sts.

Rows 1–8: Knit.

Row 9 (RS): Knit.

Row 10: K2, [p17, k4] twice.

Rows 11–32: [Rep Rows 9 and 10] 11 times. (24 rows total)

Rows 33–36: Knit.

Rows 37–288: [Rep Rows 9–36] 9 times.

Rows 289–292: Knit.

Bind off all sts.

Finishing

Sew left, right and center panel tog. Referring to charts and Fig. 1, duplicate st ornaments on afghan. ◆

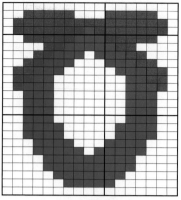

CHART A

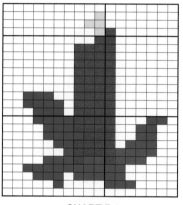

CHART B

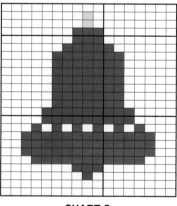

CHART C

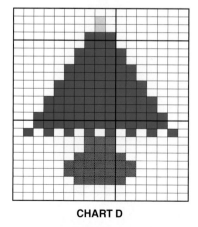

CHART D

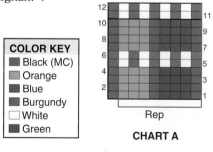

*Kente Afghan for Kwaanza
continued from page 96*

ending with a WS row.

Next row: K21, then sl these 21 sts to a holder for side border; with MC, k159, sl last 21 sts to holder for side border.

Center

Working on center 159 sts only, continue in MC and garter st until piece measures 55 inches from beg. Leave center sts on a spare needle.

Left Side Border

Sl 21 sts from st holder onto larger needle so that you are ready to beg at inside edge with a RS row. Rejoin yarns and continue in established pat until band fits side edge, ending with Row 4 or 8. Sl sts to a holder.

Right Side Border

Work in established pat to match left border, leaving sts on needle to beg top border.

Top Border

With larger needles and RS facing, work 21 sts from right border in established pat; continue in pat across next 159 sts; work 21 sts from st holder (left border).

Continue in established pat until 2 pat reps (24 rows) have been completed. Change to smaller needles and MC. Work 4 rows garter st. Bind off all sts.

Finishing

Sew side borders to main section of afghan. ◆

COLOR KEY
■ Black (MC)
■ Orange
■ Blue
■ Burgundy
☐ White
■ Green

CHART A

Christmas Forest Afghan continued from page 98

Pine Forest Afghan continued from page 106

yarn, leaving a 6-inch tail.

Square A

With white, cast on 21 sts, then pick up and k 20 sts along top edge of previous square. Knit 1 row. Work mitered square pat.

Square B

After 2nd square is completed, using same color, pick up and k 20 sts along left-hand edge of first square, then cast on 21 sts. Knit 1 row. Work mitered square pat.

After 3rd square is completed, with green, work an A square on top of square 2.

With green, work a C square between squares 2 and 3 using green.

Square C

Pick up and k 20 sts along left edge of square 2, pick up and k 1 st in corner, then pick up and k 20 sts along top edge of square 3. Knit 1 row. Work mitered square pat.

Referring to Fig. 1, continue to work squares in colors and sequence as indicated until there are 8 squares across and 9 squares high.

Border

With smaller needle and red, pick up and k 180 sts along side edge. Knit 5 rows. Bind off all sts. Rep for other side edge.

Pick up and k 166 sts along top edge, including 3 sts along edges of side borders. Knit 5 rows. Bind off all sts. Rep for bottom edge. ◆

STITCH KEY
☐ K on RS, p on WS
⊟ P on RS, k on WS
☒ Duplicate st with CC

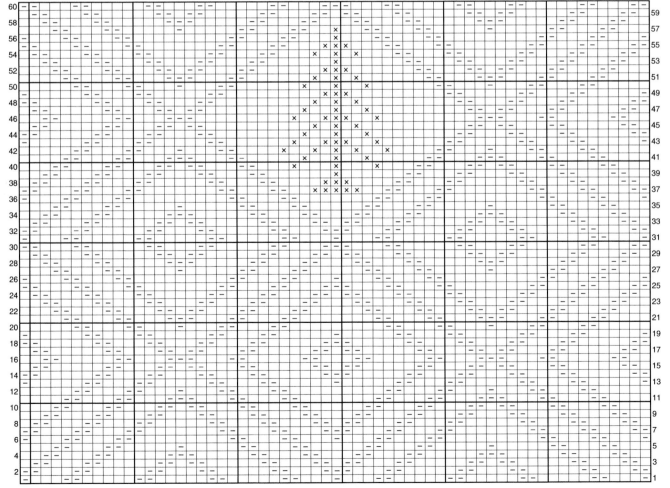

PINE FOREST AFGHAN CHART

Patchwork Pleasures

*A*fghans knit in strips and squares are easy to carry along and work on in bits and pieces of time. Whether you use scrap yarn or colorways to match your home, this collection of gorgeous afghans will brighten your home and keep you warm on cold snowy evenings.

Chapter 6

Windowpane Afghan

Design by Lois S. Young

Portable strips work up quickly and are attached in a unique way by knitting them together from the right side. Variegated yarn adds charm to this afghan.

Skill Level
Intermediate***

Finished Measurements
Approximately 46 x 61 inches

Materials
- Plymouth Encore Colorspun worsted weight 75 percent acrylic/25 percent wool yarn (200 yds/100g per ball): 11 skeins pink and blue variegated #7111 (MC)
- Plymouth Encore worsted weight 75 percent acrylic/25 percent wool yarn (200 yds/100g per ball): 7 skeins navy #848 (CC)
- Size 10 (6mm) circular needle or size needed to obtain gauge
- Stitch holders
- Tapestry needle

Gauge
11 sts = 4 inches/10cm in pat with 2 strands of yarn held tog

MC patch of 13 sts and 15 rows measures 4½ x 3½ inches

To save time, take time to check gauge.

Pattern Notes
Afghan is worked with 2 strands held tog throughout.

When working strips, make a ch selvage by sl first st on all RS rows knit-wise, and first st on all WS rows purlwise. Sl all sts with yarn on WS of fabric.

When working last row of a color, work last st in new color.

Special Abbreviation
M1 (Make 1): Inc by making a backward loop on right-hand needle.

Pattern Stitches
Strip Pat

Row 1 (WS): Sl 1, purl across.

Row 2: With MC, sl 1, k2, p1, [k3, p1] twice, end k1.

Row 3 and remaining WS rows: Sl 1, purl across.

Row 4: Sl 1, [p1, k3] 3 times.

Rows 5–16: [Rep Rows 1–4] 3 more times.

Rows 17–20: With CC, beg with a WS (purl) row, work in St st, sl first st of each row.

Rep Rows 1–20 for pat.

Seed St

Row 1: *K1, p1, rep from * across.

Row 2: *P1, k1, rep from * across.

Rep Rows 1 and 2 for an even number of sts, or Row 1 only for an odd number of sts.

Strips
Make 10

Note: On first pat rep of strip, cast on counts as Row 1.

With MC, cast on 13 sts. Beg with Row 2, work [Rows 1–20] 13 times, then rep [Rows 1–16] once. Break yarn, put sts on holder.

Joining Strips
With CC, cast on 3 sts. K2, sl 1 wyib, pick up and k 1 st from edge of RS of bottom of 1 strip, return last 2 sts to left needle and k2tog tbl, turn. Sl 1, k1, sl 1 wyif, insert tip of needle from RS to WS of fabric, pick up and p 1 st from edge of bottom of WS of a 2nd strip, turn.

Row 1: K2tog, k1, sl 1, pick up and k 1 st from edge of RS of first strip, return last 2 sts to left needle, k2tog tbl, turn.

Row 2: Sl 1, k1, sl 1 with yarn in front, pick up and p 1 st from edge of WS of 2nd strip, turn.

Rep Rows 1 and 2 until strips have been joined, put sts on holders. Join remaining strips in same manner.

Top Border
With RS facing, sl all sts on needle, join CC.

Row 1: K12, *k2tog, k1, ssk, k11, rep from * across. (138 sts)

Work 5 rows seed st. Bind off all sts in pat.

Bottom Border
With RS facing, pick up and k 11 sts in each MC part of strip, 3 sts in each joining strip. (137 sts)

Work 5 rows seed st, rep Row 1 only. Bind off all sts in pat.

Side Borders
With RS facing, *pick up and k 2 sts along sl st edge, M1, rep from *. Work border to match top and bottom, working Rows 1 and 2 of seed st pat for an even number of sts, or Row 1 only for an odd number of sts. Rep for other side. ◆

Raspberry Parfait Afghan

Design by Laura Polley

Use a basic entrelac pattern, garter stitch border and variegated yarn to create a truly beautiful afghan.

Skill Level
Advanced****

Finished Size
Approximately 52 x 58 inches blocked, before border

Materials
- Plymouth Encore Colorspun worsted weight 75 percent acrylic/25 percent wool yarn (200 yds/100g per ball): 20 balls gray and pink variegated #7990
- Size 11 (8mm) 29-inch or longer circular needle or size needed to obtain gauge
- Tapestry needle

Gauge
12½ sts and 18 rows = 4 inches/ 10cm in St st with 2 strands of yarn held tog

12 sts and 24 rows = 4 inches/ 10cm in garter st with 2 strands of yarn held tog

To save time, take time to check gauge.

Pattern Notes
Afghan is worked with 2 strands of yarn held tog throughout.

Circular needle is used to accomodate large number of sts. Do not join at end of row. Straight needles may be used for body of afghan if desired, but circular needle is recommended because of frequent turning of work.

Circular needle is also needed to work borders.

When picking up sts on WS, insert RH needle from RS to WS and p1.

Special Abbreviation
Tw: Turn work.

Entrelac Pat
1. Base Triangles
*K2, tw, p2, tw, k3, tw, p3. Continue in this manner, working 1 more st every RS row until 10 sts have been worked. Leave these 10 sts on RH needle. (1 triangle completed)

Rep from * across row.

2. Edge Triangle (WS)
P into front and back of first st, p2tog, tw, k3, tw, p into front and back of first st, pl, p2tog, tw, k4. Continue in this manner, working 1 more purl st every WS row before p2tog, until there are 10 sts on RH needle. Leave these sts on needle.

3. Right-Slanting Rectangles (WS)
With WS facing, pick up and p 10 sts along side edge of triangle just worked, sl last picked up st back to LH needle and p2tog with first st of next section, *tw, k10, tw, p9, p2tog with first st of next section, rep from * until 10 sts of section have been worked. Work across remaining sections in same manner.

4. Edge Triangle
Pick up and p 9 sts along side edge of last triangle, tw, k9, tw, p7, p2tog, tw, k8. Continue to work in this manner, p2tog at end of every WS row until 1 st remaining, tw.

5. Left-Slanting Rectangles (RS)
Sl remaining st of edge triangle purlwise onto RH needle. Pick up and k 9

sts along side of edge triangle just worked, kl from first rectangle, sl last st picked up over it, *tw, p10, tw, k9, sl 1, kl from rectangle, psso, rep from * until all 10 sts from first rectangle have been worked and there are 10 sts on RH needle. Leave sts on RH needle. Pick up and k 10 sts along side edge of next rectangle. Rep from * across row.

Rep Steps 2–5 for entrelac pat.

With 2 strands of yarn held tog, loosely cast on 110 sts. Work Steps 1–5 of entrelac pat, then [rep Steps 2–5] 10 times more.

Finishing Triangles (WS)
P into front and back of first st, p2tog, tw, k3, tw, p into front and back of first st, pl, p2tog, tw, k4. Continue in this manner, adding 1 more purl st every WS row before p2tog, until you work k6.

Next row (WS): P2tog, p3, p2tog, tw, k5, tw, p2tog, p2, p2tog, tw, k4, tw, p2tog, pl, p2tog, tw, k3, tw, [p2tog] twice, tw, k2, tw, p2tog. (1 st remaining)

*Pick up and p 10 sts, tw, k11, tw, p2tog, p8, p2tog, tw, k10, tw. Continue in this manner, p2tog at each side of WS rows, end p3tog (1 st remaining)

Rep from *, work last triangle as follows: on side edge, pick up and p 9 sts, tw, k10, tw, p2tog at beg and end of WS row without joining. Continue in this manner, end p2 tog. Fasten off last st.

Finishing
Block afghan.

Side Borders
With RS facing, beg at right corner

Continued on page 133

Patchwork Trio Afghan

Design by Diane Zangl

Large needles, basic stitches—stockinette, seed and cable—and a checkerboard arrangement best show the texture of this fast-knitting project.

Skill Level
Beginner*

Size
Approximately 40 x 50 inches (blocked)

Materials
- Plymouth Encore worsted weight 75 percent acrylic/25 percent wool yarn (200 yds/100g per ball): 4 balls each plum #959 (A), dark mauve #958 (B), dusty rose #2340 (C)
- Size 11 (7mm) needle or size needed to obtain gauge
- Cable needle
- Tapestry needle

Gauge
13 sts and 16 rows = 4 inches/10cm in St st with 2 strands of yarn held tog

To save time, take time to check gauge.

Pattern Notes
Afghan is worked with 2 strands of yarn held tog throughout. Use 2 strands for sewing squares tog.

If desired, afghan may be knit in 4 panels of 5 squares each. Refer to Fig. 1 for sequence, do not bind off after each square is completed. Cut old color, join new color at beg of next row. Work as directed for next square.

Special Abbreviation
C6 (Cable 6): Sl 3 sts to cn and hold in front, k3, k3 from cn.

Square 1
Make 7

With 2 strands of A, cast on 32 sts. Knit 3 rows.

Row 1 (RS): Knit.

Row 2: K3, p to last 3 sts, k3.

[Rep Rows 1 and 2] 19 times more. Knit 4 rows. Bind off all sts.

Square 2
Make 6

With 2 strands of B, cast on 32 sts. Knit 3 rows.

Row 1 (RS): K3, p2, [k2, p2] 6 times, k3.

Rows 2 and 3: K5, [p2, k2] 6 times, k3.

Row 4: Rep Row 1.

[Rep Rows 1–4] 9 times more. Knit 4 rows. Bind off all sts.

Square 3
Make 7

With 2 strands of C, cast on 32 sts. Knit 3 rows.

Rows 1 and 5 (RS): [K6, p1] twice, k4, [p1, k6] twice.

Rows 2, 4 and 6: K3, p3, k1, p6, k1, p4, k1, p6, k1, p3, k3.

Row 3: K6, p1, C6, p1, k4, p1, C6, p1, k6.

[Rep Rows 1–6] 5 times more. Work
Continued on page 133

Counterpane Log Afghan

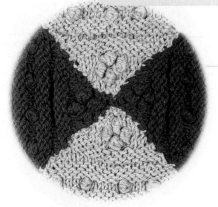

Design By Fatema Habibur-Rahman

You'll enjoy stitching this portable project that comes alive when assembled. Knit the triangles individually, sew them into squares and combine the squares.

Skill Level
Easy**

Finished Size
Approximately 40 x 48 inches

Materials
- Plymouth Encore worsted weight 75 percent acrylic/25 percent wool yarn (200 yds/100g per ball): 5 balls each beige #1415, dark rose #180
- Size 10 (6mm) needles or size needed to obtain gauge
- Tapestry needle

Gauge
18 sts and 20 rows = 4 inches/10cm

To save time, take time to check gauge

Special Abbreviations
MB (Make Bobble): In next st [k1, yo, k1, yo, k1, yo, k1], pass 2nd, 3rd, 4th, 5th, 6th, and 7th sts, 1 at a time, over first st.

M1 (Make 1): Inc by knitting in top of st in row below st on needle.

Counterpane Triangles Pattern
Make 60 triangles in each color (120 triangles)

Cast on 3 sts

Row 1 (RS): K3.

Row 2: P3.

Row 3: M1, k3, M1. (5 sts)

Row 4: Purl.

Row 5: M1, k5, M1. (7 sts)

Row 6: Purl.

Row 7: M1, k3, MB, k3, M1. (9 sts)

Row 8: Purl.

Row 9: M1, k3, MB, k1, MB, k3, M1. (11 sts)

Row 10: Purl.

Row 11: M1, k5, MB, k5, M1. (13 sts)

Row 12: Purl.

Row 13: M1, p13, M1. (15 sts)

Row 14: Knit.

Row 15: M1, p15, M1. (17 sts)

Row 16: Purl.

Row 17: M1, k17, M1. (19 sts)

Row 18: Purl.

Row 19: M1, p19, M1. (21 sts)

Row 20: Knit.

Row 21: M1, p21, M1. (23 sts)

Row 22: Purl.

Row 23: M1, k5, MB, k3, MB, k3, MB, k3, MB, k5, M1. (25 sts)

Row 24: Purl.

Row 25: M1, p25, M1. (27 sts)

Row 26: Knit.

Row 27: M1, p27, M1. (29 sts)

Row 28: Purl.

Bind off all sts.

Finishing
Referring to photo, sew 4 triangles (2 of each color) into a square, alternating colors. (30 squares)

Block squares severely. Each square should measure approximately 8 x 8 inches.

Sew squares tog, 5 squares wide by 6 squares high. ◆

Triangles on Point

Design by Carol May

Circular construction turns triangles into a square in this fantastic afghan.

Skill Level
Intermediate***

Finished Size
Approximately 48 x 48 inches

Materials
- Plymouth Encore worsted weight 75 percent acrylic/25 percent wool yarn (200 yds/100g per ball): 6 balls white #208 (A)
- Plymouth Encore Colorspun worsted weight 75 percent acrylic/25 percent wool yarn (200 yds/100g per ball): 4 balls camel drift #7357 (B)
- Size 9 (5.5mm) double-pointed needles (set of 5) and 4 (29-inch) circular needles or size needed to obtain gauge
- Stitch markers
- Tapestry needle

Gauge
20 sts = 4 inches/10cm in pat

To save time, take time to check gauge.

Pattern Notes
Afghan is worked from center out, beg on dpn, changing to circular needle

when there are enough sts. When changing to circular needle, place markers between sections. As project gets larger, it will be helpful to divide sts among several circular needles.

Each line of instructions should be rep 4 times, once for each section. Last rep of sl 1, k3 in each section will not always come out even, pat may end sl 1, k1 or k2. Sl st moves 1 st to right each time.

Beg at center with A, cast on 12 sts, leaving a 6-inch tail to close center. Divide sts so there are 3 sts on each of 4 dpn and mark beg of rnd. Join without twisting.

Rnd 1: Knit.

Rnd 2: K1, yo, k to last st, yo, k1.

Rnds 3–8: Rep Rnds 1 and 2 until there are 11 sts on each needle. (44 sts total)

Rnd 9: With B, knit, drop B at end of rnd.

Rnd 10: With A, k1, yo, *sl 1, k3, rep from * to last st, yo, k1.

Rnd 11: Knit around, sl all previously sl sts.

Rnds 12 and 14: Rep Rnd 2.

Rnd 13: Knit.

Rep Rnds 9–14 until afghan measures approximately 46½ inches across, or 1½ inches less than desired size, ending with Rnd 11. Cut B.

Edging
Rnd 1: K1, yo, [k1, p1] to last st of section, yo, k1.

Rnd 2: K1, [p1, k1] across section.

Rnd 3: K1, yo, p1, [k1, p1] to last st, yo, p1.

Rnd 4: K2, p1, [k1, p1] to last 2 sts, k2.

Rep Rnds 1–4 until edging measures 1½ inches. Bind off in pat.

Using tail from cast on, close hole in center. Block lightly. ◆

Tibetan Check Afghan

Design by Barbara Venishnick

A checkerboard is overlaid with bands of horizontal garter stitch, giving a three-dimensional effect. The afghan is constructed in one piece using intarsia technique.

Skill Level
Easy**

Finished Size
Approximately 49 x 63 inches

Materials
- Plymouth Encore worsted weight 75 percent acrylic/25 percent wool yarn (200 yds/100g per ball): 5 balls rose heather #433 (A), 4 balls each beige heather #1415 (B), grey heather #389 (C)
- Size 10 (6mm) 40-inch circular needle or size needed to obtain gauge
- Size H/8 (5mm) crochet hook (for cast on)
- Tapestry needle

Gauge
15 sts and 26 rows = 4 inches/10cm in pat

To save time, take time to check gauge.

Pattern Notes
Afghan is worked using intarsia technique. Attach separate ball of yarn for each square of checkerboard. Keep them all in a basket to avoid tangling. When changing colors, pick up new color under old to avoid holes.

Carry colors B and C up behind color A stripes. Cut yarn and reposition colors only when color B and C blocks change position. Color A may be carried up side when not in use.

Circular needle is used to accomodate large number of sts. Do not join at end of row.

Special Abbreviations
M1 (Make 1): Inc by lifting running thread between st just knit and next st onto LH needle. K1 in back loop.

Provisional cast on: With crochet hook and scrap yarn, loosely ch number of sts needed for afghan plus a few more. With working needle and afghan yarn, pick up 1 st in each purl bump on back side of ch. Ch can be undone leaving live sts to work trim. This makes a more flexible edge than a regular cast on.

With crochet hook, ch 176 sts plus a few extra. With circular needle, provisionally cast on as follows: [22 B, 22 C] 4 times.

Note: *Cast-on row counts as Row 1 of first rep of pat.*

Pattern
Row 1: Knit [22 B, 22 C] 4 times.

Row 2: Purl [22 C, 22 B] 4 times.

Rows 3 and 4: Rep Rows 1 and 2.

Rows 5–8: With A, k176.

Rows 9–40: [Rep Rows 1–8] 4 more times to complete row of checks.

Row 41: Knit [22 C, 22 B] 4 times.

Row 42: Purl [22 B, 22 C] 4 times.

Rows 43 and 44: Rep Rows 41 and 42.

Rows 45–48: With A, k176.

Rows 49–80: [Rep Rows 41–80] 4 more times to complete row of checks.

Rep [Rows 1–80] 4 times more, ending last rep with Row 76. Do not work last 4 rows of A. Finished grid will be 8 blocks wide and 10 blocks high. Do not bind off.

Top Border
Rows 1 and 2: With A, knit.

Row 3: With C, k1, M1, k to last st, M1, k1.

Row 4: With C, knit.

Rows 5 and 6: With A, knit.

Rows 7 and 8: With B, rep Rows 3 and 4.

Row 9: With A, knit.

With A, bind off all sts knitwise.

Bottom Border
Undo crochet ch and place all sts on needle. (**KnitTip:** *Undo 1 st at a time and sl resulting st onto needle as you go.*) Work as for top border.

Side Borders
With A and circular needle, pick up and k 1 st in every other row along side of afghan, with first st in first color A row of top border, and last st in first color A row of bottom border.

Row 1: With A, knit.

Row 2: With C, pick up and k 1 st in color C row of top border, knit across, pick up and k 1 st in color C row of bottom border.

Row 3: With C, knit.

Row 4: With A, pick up and k 1 st in 2nd color A row of top border, knit across, pick up and k 1 st in 2nd color A row of bottom border.

Row 5: With A, knit.

Row 6: With B, pick up and k 1 st in color B row of top border, knit across, pick up and k 1 st in color B row of bottom border.

Row 7: With B, knit.

Row 8: With A, pick up and k 1 st in last color A row of top border, knit across, pick up and k 1 st in last color A row of bottom border.

With A, bind off all sts knitwise. Rep on other side.

Block lightly. ◆

Trip-Round-the-World Afghan

Design by Elizabeth Mattfield

Simple pattern stitches, easy enough for a beginner, combine with color to make an outstanding project.

Skill Level
Easy**

Finished Size
Approximately 48 x 48 inches

Materials
- Plymouth Wildflower DK weight 51 percent mercerized cotton/49 percent acrylic yarn (136 yds/50g per ball): 4 balls aran #40 (A), 6 balls light green #42 (B), 6 balls green #49 (C), 2 balls red #46 (D), 4 balls blue #57 (E), 2 balls orange #56 (F), 3 balls lavender #50 (G), 1 ball yellow #48 (H)
- Size 10 (6mm) needles or size needed to obtain gauge
- Tapestry needle

Gauge
13 sts = 4 inches/10cm in St st with 2 strands of yarn

12 sts = 4 inches/10cm in seed st with 2 strands of yarn

To save time, take time to check gauge.

Pattern Notes
Afghan is worked with 2 strands of yarn held tog throughout.

Project shown was knitted in strips, then sewn tog. If you prefer to work afghan in 1 piece, using intarsia method, be careful to twist yarns tog at color changes to avoid holes.

Work strips with colors as given in Fig. 1, then assemble in order shown.

G	E	C	B	A	B	C	B	A	B	C	E	G
E	C	B	A	B	C	E	C	B	A	B	C	E
C	B	A	B	C	E	G	E	C	B	A	B	C
B	A	B	C	E	G	D	G	E	C	B	A	B
A	B	C	E	G	D	F	D	G	E	C	B	A
B	C	E	G	D	F	H	F	D	G	E	C	B
C	E	G	D	F	H	A	H	F	D	G	E	C
B	C	E	G	D	F	H	F	D	G	E	C	B
A	B	C	E	G	D	F	D	G	E	C	B	A
B	A	B	C	E	G	D	G	E	C	B	A	B
C	B	A	B	C	E	G	E	C	B	A	B	C
E	C	B	A	B	C	E	C	B	A	B	C	E
G	E	C	B	A	B	C	B	A	B	C	E	G

Outer strip · Strip 2 · Strip 4 · Strip 6 · Strip 6 · Strip 4 · Strip 2 · Outer strip
Strip 3 · Strip 5 · Strip 7 · Strip 5 · Strip 3

FIG. 1

Colors A, C and G are always worked in seed st; B, D, E, F and H are always worked in St st. St st blocks are 1 st wider than seed st blocks, so inc or dec 1 st near center of block as needed when changing colors. Seed st blocks are 20 rows long, St st blocks are 18 rows long.

Pattern Stitch
Seed St (even number of sts)

Row 1: *K1, p1, rep from * across.

Row 2: *P1, k1, rep from * across.

Rep Rows 1 and 2 for pat.

Outer Strip
Make 2

Referring to Fig. 1, cast on 14 sts and work in color and pat sequence as given, sl first st on 1 edge throughout until 13 blocks have been completed. Bind off in pat.

Rep for other edge strip, sl st on opposite edge.

COLOR KEY
Aran (A)
Light green (B)
Green (C)
Red (D)
Blue (E)
Orange (F)
Lavender (G)
Yellow (H)

Continued on page 133

Inside Out Afghan

Design by Katharine Hunt

This romantic afghan is sure to become a cherished heirloom. The squares are worked from the center out on double-pointed needles.

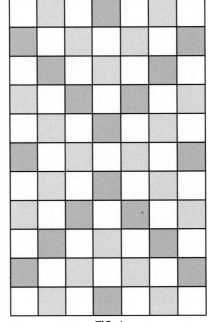

FIG. 1

COLOR KEY
☐ Aran (A)
▨ Pale blue (B)
▨ Sage green (C)

Skill Level
Advanced****

Finished Size
Approximately 42 x 66 inches, lightly blocked without border; each square measures approximately 6 inches

Materials
• Plymouth Encore worsted weight 75 percent acrylic/25 percent wool yarn (200 yds/100g per ball): 7 balls Aran #256 (A), 3 balls each pale blue #514 (B), sage green #1231 (C)
• Size 6 (4mm) double-pointed needles (set of 5) or size needed to obtain gauge
• Tapestry needle

Gauge
20 sts = 4 inches/10cm in St st
To save time, take time to check gauge.

Pattern Notes
Squares are worked from center out, on 4 dpn, working with 5th needle. Each line of instructions should be rep 4 times, once on each needle.

Careful assembly is essential so pats line up from square to square.

Special Abbreviation
Sl 1-k: Slip 1 knitwise

Squares
Make 77 squares: 39 A, 20 B and 18 C.

Cast on 8 sts and distribute evenly on 4 needles.

Rnd 1 and remaining odd-numbered rnds through 19: Knit.

Rnd 2: [Yo, k1] twice.

Rnd 4: Yo, k3, yo, k1.

Rnd 6: Yo, k5, yo, k1.

Rnd 8: Yo, k7, yo, k1.

Rnd 10: Yo, k4, yo, ssk, k3, yo, k1.

Rnd 12: Yo, k3, k2tog, yo, k1, yo, ssk, k3, yo, k1.

Rnd 14: Yo, k3, k2tog, yo, k3, yo, ssk, k3, yo, k1.

Rnd 16: Yo, k3, k2tog, yo, k5, yo, ssk, k3, yo, k1.

Rnd 18: Yo, k3, k2tog, yo, k7, yo, ssk, k3, yo, k1.

Rnd 20: Yo, p19, yo, p1.

Rnd 21: *K2tog, yo, rep from * arouind.

Rnd 22: P1, yo, p20, yo, p1.

Bind off knitwise, keeping last st on needle.

Close off corner
With last st still on needle, pick up, then bind off one st on each side of corner (2nd st is just before original bind-off st). With final st still on needle, thread yarn tail in tapestry needle. Bring point of tapestry needle up through 2 strands of original bind-off st, then up through final st on needle, removing it from needle. Push needle back down where it came up, securing st.

Finishing
Block squares to size.

Referring to Fig. 1, assemble squares as shown, using A for stitching.

Joining squares
Lay 1 square on top of another, with RS facing, matching openwork pat exactly, and st from back. Pat on each square must be aligned exactly with the adjacent square. For best alignment, begin stitching squares in center of edges to be sewn, leaving a tail of yarn. Work st for st from center to corner, then using yarn tail, work from center to remaining corner.

Border
Make diagonal corner
With A, cast on 7 sts. *K7, turn, k5, turn, yb, sl 1-k, k4, turn, k3, turn, yb, sl 1-k, k2, turn, k1, put last k st back on LH needle, k7.**

Edging
Row 1(RS): K1, k2tog, [yo] twice,

Continued on page 133

Diagonal Squares Afghan

Design by Katharine Hunt

With the look of counterpanes, this lovely two-toned afghan will be a pleasure to knit.

Skill Level
Intermediate***

Finished Size
Approximately 48 x 64 inches, lightly blocked without border: each square measures approximately 8 inches

Materials
- Plymouth Encore worsted weight 75 percent acrylic/25 percent wool yarn (200 yds/100g per ball): 9 balls pale sage green #1231 (A), 7 balls dark sage green #1232 (B)
- Size 7 (4.5mm) needles or size needed to obtain gauge
- Tapestry needle

Gauge
20 sts = 4 inches/10cm in St st
To save time, take time to check gauge.

Pattern Note
Squares are worked from corner to corner, changing colors at middle, then seamed tog. Edging is worked separately, then sewn to edges.

Special Abbreviations
MB (Make Bobble): [K1, p1] twice into next st, turn; p4, turn; sl 2nd st over first st, return st to RH needle, on LH needle, pass 2nd st over first st, put st from RH needle back on LH needle, k2tog tbl.

Sl 1-k: Slip 1 knitwise.

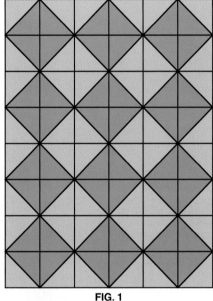

FIG. 1

Square
Make 48

Inc side

With B, cast on 2 sts.
Row 1: Sl 1, yo, k1. (3 sts)
Row 2: Sl 1, k2.
Row 3: Sl 1, [yo, k1] twice. (5 sts)
Row 4: Sl 1, k4.
Row 5: Sl 1, yo, k3, yo, k1. (7 sts)
Row 6: Sl 1, k6.
Row 7: Sl 1, yo, k5, yo, k1. (9 sts)
Row 8: Sl 1, k8.
Row 9: Sl 1, yo, k7, yo, k1. (11 sts)
Row 10: Sl 1, k10.
Row 11: Sl 1, yo, k9, yo, k1. (13 sts)
Row 12: Sl 1, k12.
Row 13: Sl 1, yo, k11, yo, k1. (15 sts)
Row 14: Sl 1, p13, k1.
Row 15: Sl 1, yo, [k1, p2] 4 times, k1, yo, k1. (17 sts)

Row 16: Sl 1, k1, p1, [k2, p1] 4 times, k2.
Row 17: Sl 1, yo, p1, [k1, p2] 4 times, k1, p1, yo, k1. (19 sts)
Row 18: Sl 1, [k2, p1] 5 times, k3.
Row 19: Sl 1, yo, k17, yo, k1. (21 sts)
Row 20: Sl 1, p19, k1.
Row 21: Sl 1, yo, k19, yo, k1. (23 sts)
Row 22: Sl 1, k22.
Row 23: Sl 1, yo, k21, yo, k1. (25 sts)
Row 24: Sl 1, k24.
Row 25: Sl 1, yo, k23, yo, k1. (27 sts)
Row 26: Sl 1, k26.
Row 27: Sl 1, yo, k25, yo, k1. (29 sts)
Row 28: Sl 1, p27, k1.
Row 29: Sl 1, yo, k27, yo, k1. (31 sts)
Row 30: Sl 1, k30.
Row 31: Sl 1, yo, k1, [yo, k2tog] to last st, yo, k1. (33 sts)
Row 32: Sl 1, k32.
Row 33: Sl 1, yo, k31, yo, k1. (35 sts)
Row 34: Sl 1, p33, k1.
Row 35: Sl 1, yo, k1, [MB, k4] 6 times, MB, k1, yo, k1. (37 sts)
Row 36: Sl 1, p35, k1.
Row 37: Sl 1, yo, p35, yo, k1. (39 sts)
Row 38: Sl 1, p38.
Row 39: Sl 1, yo, k1, [yo, k2tog] to last st, yo, k1. (41 sts)
Row 40: Sl 1, k40.
Row 41: Sl 1, yo, k39, yo, k1. (43 sts)
Row 42: Sl 1, p41, k1.
Row 43: Sl 1, yo, k41, yo, k1. (45 sts)
Row 44: Sl 1, k44.
Row 45: Sl 1, yo, k43, yo, k1. (47sts)
Row 46: Sl 1, k46.
Row 47: Sl 1, yo, k45, yo, k1. (49 sts)
Row 48: Sl 1, k48.

Row 49: Sl 1, yo, k47, yo, k1. (51 sts)

Row 50: Sl 1, p49, k1.

Row 51: Sl 1, yo, k49, yo, k1. (53 sts)

Dec Side

Change to A.

Row 52: Sl 1, p51, k1.

Row 53: Sl 1, ssk, k47, k2tog, k1. (51 sts)

Row 54: Sl 1, p49, k1.

Row 55: Sl 1, ssk, k45, k2tog, k1. (49 sts)

Row 56: Sl 1, k to end.

Row 57: Sl 1, ssk, k43, k2tog, k1. (47 sts)

Row 58: Sl 1, k to end.

Row 59: Sl 1, ssk, k41, k2tog, k1. (45 sts)

Row 60: Sl 1, k to end.

Row 61: Sl 1, ssk, k39, k2tog, k1. (43 sts)

Row 62: Sl 1, p to last st, k1.

Row 63: Sl 1, ssk, k37, k2tog, k1. (41 sts)

Row 64: Sl 1, k to end.

Row 65: Sl 1, ssk, k35, k2tog, k1. (39 sts)

Row 66: Sl 1, k to end.

Row 67: Sl 1, ssk, k33, k2tog, k1. (37 sts)

Row 68: Sl 1, k to end.

Row 69: Sl 1, ssk, k31, k2tog, k1. (35 sts)

Row 70: Sl 1, k to end.

Row 71: Sl 1, ssk, k29, k2tog, k1. (33 sts)

Row 72: Sl 1, k to end.

Row 73: Sl 1, ssk, k27, k2tog, k1. (31 sts)

Row 74: Sl 1, k to end.

Row 75: Sl 1, ssk, k25, k2tog, k1. (29 sts)

Row 76: Sl 1, p to last st, k1.

Row 77: Sl 1, ssk, k23, k2tog, k1. (27 sts)

Row 78: Sl 1, k to end.

Row 79: Sl 1, ssk, k21, k2tog, k1. (25 sts)

Row 80: Sl 1, k to end.

Row 81: Sl 1, ssk, k19, k2tog, k1. (23 sts)

Row 82: Sl 1, k to end.

Row 83: Sl 1, ssk, k17, k2tog, k1. (21 sts)

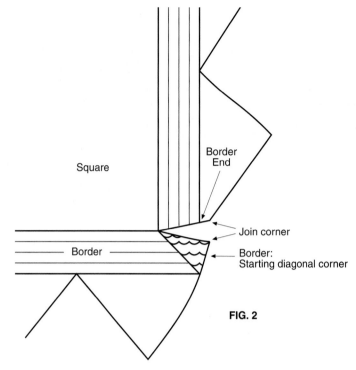

FIG. 2

Row 84: Sl 1, p to last st, k1.

Row 85: Sl 1, ssk, p1, [k1, p2] 4 times, k1, p1, k2tog, k1. (19 sts)

Row 86: Sl 1, p1, k1, [p1, k2] 4 times, [p1, k1] twice.

Row 87: Sl 1, ssk, [k1, p2] 4 times, k1, k2tog, k1. (17 sts)

Row 88: Sl 1, p2, [k2, p1] 4 times, p1, k1.

Row 89: Sl 1, ssk, k11, k2tog, k1. (15 sts)

Row 90: Sl 1, p13, k1.

Row 91: Sl 1, ssk, k9, k2tog, k1. (13 sts)

Row 92: Sl 1, k to end.

Row 93: Sl 1, ssk, k7, k2tog, k1. (11 sts)

Row 94: Sl 1, k to end.

Row 95: Sl 1, ssk, k5, k2tog, k1. (9 sts)

Row 96: Sl 1, k to end.

Row 97: Sl 1, ssk, k3, k2tog, k1. (7 sts)

Row 98: Sl 1, p to last st, k1.

Row 99: Sl 1, ssk, MB, k2tog, k1. (5 sts)

Row 100: Sl 1, p3, k1.

Row 101: Ssk, k1, k2tog. (3 sts)

Row 102: Sl 1, k2tog.

Bind off last 2 sts.

Finishing

Block squares to size.

Referring to Fig. 1, assemble squares, seaming from front.

Border

*Make starting diagonal corner.

With A, cast on 9 sts. K9, turn; k7, turn; yb, sl 1-k, k6, turn; k5, turn; yb, sl 1-k, k4, turn; k3, turn; yb, sl 1-k, k2, turn; k9.

Edging

Row 1(RS): K2, [yo, k2tog] twice, yo, k3.

Row 2 and all even rows: Knit.

Row 3: K2, [yo, k2tog] twice, yo, k4.

Row 5: K2, [yo, k2tog] twice, yo, k5.

Row 7: K2, [yo, k2tog] twice, yo, k6.

Row 9: K2, [yo, k2tog] twice, yo, k7.

Row 11: K2, [yo, k2tog] twice, yo, k8.

Row 13: K2, [yo, k2tog] twice, yo, k9.

Row 15: K2, [yo, k2tog] twice, yo, k10.

Row 17: K2, [yo, k2tog] twice, yo, k11.

Row 18: Bind off 9 sts, k8.

On final Row 18, bind off all sts.

Rep Rows 1–18 until edging, very slightly stretched, measures same as side of afghan. There should be 3 border points for each square.

Rep corner and edging from * for remaining 3 sides. Sew borders to afghan edges. Sew corner seams. ◆

*Raspberry Parfait Afghan
continued from page 116*

*Trip-Round-the-World Afghan
continued from page 126*

*Inside Out Afghan
Continued from page 128*

of side of afghan, with 2 strands of yarn, pick up and k 173 sts along side of afghan. (15 sts per complete entrelac section, and 8 sts per half-section)

Knit 5 rows. Bind off knitwise on RS. Rep across opposite side.

Upper Border

With RS facing, beg at right corner of bind-off edge, with 2 strands of yarn, pick up and k 4 sts from edge of side border, 154 sts across bind-off edge of afghan (14 sts per complete entrelac section and 7 sts per half-section), and 4 sts from edge of 2nd side border. (162 sts total)

Complete as for side borders, sl first st purlwise wyif on every row, including bind-off row.

Lower Border

Work as for upper border, picking up from cast-on edge of afghan and remaining edges of side borders. ◆

Strips 2–6
Make 2 of each

Cast on in color as shown at bottom of Fig. 1 for each strip, 13 sts for seed st squares, 14 sts for St st squares. Do not sl edge sts. Work as given until 13 blocks have been completed. Bind off in pat.

Strip 7

Center, make 1

With C, cast on 13 sts and work as shown until 13 blocks have been completed. Do not sl edge sts. Bind off in pat.

Finishing

Referring to Fig. 1, sew strips tog. ◆

k2tog, [yo] twice, k2.

Row 2: K3, [p1, k2] twice.

Row 3: K1, k2tog, [yo] twice, k2tog, k4.

Row 4: Bind off 2 sts, k3, p1, k2.

Rep Rows 1–4 until length of edging, very slightly stretched, fits length of 1 side of afghan. For best fit, work edging to within a few inches of correct length, sew to edge of assembled afghan, then complete remaining length of edging, ending with Row 4, then work diagonal corner from * to **. Bind off remaining sts.

Rep for other 3 sides. Sew diagonal corner seams. ◆

*Patchwork Trio Afghan
continued from page 118*

Rows 1–4.
Knit 4 rows.
Bind off.

Finishing

Referring to Fig. 1, sew squares tog as shown. Block. ◆

2	3	1	2
1	2	3	1
3	1	2	3
2	3	1	2
1	2	3	1

FIG. 1

Cozy Comforts

C *url up on those cool winter nights with these attractive afghans rich with texture and cables. As beautiful as they are warm, they are designed to soothe you, body and soul.*

Chapter 7

Homespun Stripes

Design by Edie Eckman

Knit this comfy afghan in your favorite colors, using chunky yarn. It's sure to please any member of the family.

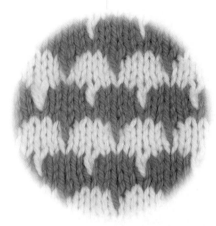

Skill Level
Beginner*

Finished Size
Approximately 46 x 59 inches

Materials
- Plymouth Encore Chunky bulky weight 75 percent acrylic/25 percent wool yarn (143 yds/100g per ball): 7 balls blue #515 (A), 6 balls natural #256 (B)
- Size 10 (6mm) 29- or 36-inch circular needle
- Tapestry needle

Gauge
13 sts and 19 rows = 4 inches/10cm in pat

To save time, take time to check gauge.

Pattern Notes
Circular needle is used to accomodate large number of sts. Do not join at end of row.

Measure length by holding piece vertically; weight of afghan will make it stretch.

Afghan
With A, cast on 139 sts. Knit 5 rows, ending with a WS row. (3 ridges garter st)

Rows 1 and 3 (RS): With B, knit.

Rows 2 and 4: With B, purl.

Row 5: With A, k3, *put tip of RH needle into next st in first row of B, pull up loop, k1, pass loop over st just knitted, k3, rep from * across.

Rows 6 and 8: With A, purl.

Row 7: With A, knit.

Row 9: With B, k1, * put tip of RH needle into next st in first row of A, pull up loop, k1, pass loop over st just knitted, k3, rep from *, ending last rep k1 instead of k3.

Rows 10 and 12: With B, purl.

Row 11: With B, knit.

Rep Rows 5–12 for pat until afghan measures approximately 57 inches from beg, ending with Row 5 of pat. With A, knit 5 rows. Bind off all sts.

Side Border
*With A, pick up and k 215 sts along long edge of afghan. Knit 5 rows. Bind off all sts. Rep from * for other side. ◆

Cross-Stitch Squares

Design by Joyce Englund

This traditional design features the checkerboard effect of cross-stitch squares and stockinette stitch. Each square is surrounded by knit stitches.

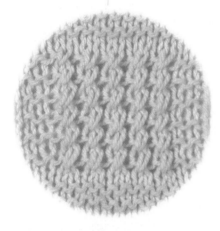

Special Abbreviation

Right Twist (RT): K1 in front of 2nd st on LH needle, k1 in back of first st on LH needle, sl both sts off needle at once.

Afghan

Cast on 142 sts. Work 4 ridges of garter st, ending with a RS row, and placing a marker 6 sts from each end for side borders.

Row 1 (WS): K6, p to 2nd marker, k6.

Row 2: K6, [RT] 5 times (10 sts), *p2, k10, p2, [RT] 5 times, rep from * to marker, end k6.

Rows 3–12: [Rep Rows 1 and 2] 5 times.

Row 13: Rep Row 1.

Rows 14–18: Knit.

Row 19: K6, p to 2nd marker, k6.

Row 20: K16, *p2, [RT] 5 times, p2, k10, rep from * to marker, end k6.

Skill Level

Easy**

Finished Size

Approximately 48 x 56 inches

Materials

• Plymouth Encore Chunky bulky weight 75 percent acrylic/25 percent wool yarn (143 yds/100g per ball): 11 balls butter yellow #215
• Size 11 (8mm) 29-inch circular needle or size needed to obtain gauge
• Stitch markers
• Tapestry needle

Gauge

12 sts and 16 rows = 4 inches/ 10cm in St st

To save time, take time to check gauge.

Rows 21–30: [Rep Rows 19 and 20] 5 times.

Row 31: Rep Row 19.

Rows 32–36: Knit.

Rows 37–216: [Rep Rows 1–36] 5 times.

Rows 217–229: [Rep Rows 1–13] once. Remove markers.

Knit 8 rows. Bind off all sts knitwise on RS. ◆

Eyelet Lace Afghan

Design by Shari Haux

Cables and lace are combined with a simple garter stitch edge to create this dramatic but delicate throw.

Skill Level
Intermediate***

Finished Size
Approximately 49¼ x 58½ inches

Materials
- Plymouth Encore worsted weight 75 percent acrylic/25 percent wool yarn (200 yds/100g per ball): 9 balls blue #515
- Size 8 (5mm) 29-inch circular needle or size needed to obtain gauge
- Stitch markers
- Cable needle
- Tapestry needle

Gauge
17 sts and 24 rows = 4 inches/10cm in St st

To save time, take time to check gauge.

Pattern Notes
Circular needle is used to accomodate large number of sts. Do not join at end of row.

To help keep track of pat reps, designer suggests placing a marker after each rep.

Special Abbreviation
BC (Back Cross): Sl next 3 sts to cn, hold in back, k3, k3 from cn.

Afghan
Cast on 193 sts and knit 8 rows (4 ridges of garter st). Place a marker 6 sts in from each edge and work these sts in garter st throughout.

Row 1 (RS): K6, *yo, ssk, k1, k2tog, yo, k6, rep from * to last 11 sts, yo, ssk, k1, k2tog, yo, k6.

Row 2, 4 and 6: K6, p to last 6 sts, k6.

Row 3: K6, *k1, yo, sl 1, k2tog, psso, yo, k7, rep from * to last 11 sts, k1, yo, sl 1, k2tog, psso, yo, k7.

Row 5: K6, *yo, ssk, k1, k2tog, yo, k6, rep from * to last 11 sts, yo, ssk, k1, k2tog, yo, k6.

Row 7: K6, *k1, yo, sl 1, k2tog, psso, yo, k1, BC, rep from * to last 11 sts, k1, yo, sl 1, k2tog, psso, yo, k7.

Row 8: Rep Row 2.

Rep Rows 1–8 for pat until piece measures 57¼ inches from beg.

Knit 8 rows. Bind off all sts. ◆

Cables & Fans Afghan

Design by Katharine Hunt

Cables and fans worked up in panels combine into a cozy afghan. Encore yarn is available in so many shades that you're sure to find just the right color for your home.

Skill Level

Intermediate***

Finished Size

Approximately 53 x 59¼ inches

Materials

- Plymouth Encore worsted weight 75 percent acrylic/25 percent wool yarn (200 yds/100g per ball): 13 balls olive green #1552
- Size 6 (4mm) straight and 29-inch circular needles or size needed to obtain gauge
- Cable needle
- Stitch holders or waste yarn
- Tapestry needle

Gauge

20 sts = 4 inches/10cm in St st

To save time, take time to check gauge.

Special Abbreviation

MB (Make Bobble): [K1, p1] twice in next st, turn; p4, turn; [k2tog tbl] twice, push bobble out from back to make round shape, pass 2nd st over first st, pull tight.

Pattern Stitches

Fan Pat (panel of 29 sts, inc to 45 sts)

Afghan

Cast on 29 sts.

Row 1 (RS): K2, yo, k1, [p2, k1] 8 times, yo, k2. (31 sts)

Row 2: K3, p1, [k2, p1] 8 times, k3.

Row 3: K3, yo, k1, [p2, k1] 8 times, yo, k3. (33 sts)

Row 4: K4, p1, [k2, p1] 8 times, k4.

Rows 5–16: Continue to work in this manner, inc 1 st on each side every RS row. Row 16 will beg and end k10. (45 sts)

Row 17: K10, [sl 1 knitwise wyib, p2tog, psso] 4 times, k1, [p2tog, yb, sl st back to LH needle, pass 2nd st over, return st to RH needle] 4 times. (29 sts)

Row 18: Knit.

Row 19: K10, *[MB, k1] 5 times, k9.

Row 20: Knit.

Rep Rows 1–20 for pat.

Left Cable Pat (panel of 11 sts)

Row 1: P2, sl next st to cn and hold in back, k2, k1 from cn, k1, sl next 2 sts to cn and hold in front, k1, k2 from cn, p2.

Row 2 and all WS rows: K the knit sts and p the purl sts. Yo's from previous row are purled.

Row 3: P2, k2, yo, sl next 2 sts as if to k2tog, k1, p2sso, yo, k2, p2.

Row 5, 7, 9, 11, 13 and 15: Rep Row 3.

Row 17: P2, sl next 2 sts to cn and hold in front, p1, k2 from cn, k1, sl next st to cn and hold in back, k2, p1 from cn, p2.

Row 19: P3, sl next 3 sts to cn and hold in front, k2, sl LH st from cn to left needle, k1, k2 from cn, p3.

Row 20: Rep Row 2.

Rep Rows 1–20 for pat.

Right Cable Pat (panel of 11 sts)

Rows 1–18: Rep Rows 1–18 of left cable panel.

Row 19: P3, sl next 3 sts to cn and hold in back, k2, sl LH st from cn to left needle and k1, k2 from cn, p3.

Row 20: Rep Row 2.

Rep Rows 1–20 for pat.

Panel A

Make 4

Cast on 29 sts. [Rep Rows 1–20 of fan pat] 19 times. Place remaining 29 sts on a st holder or length of yarn.

Panel B

Make 3

Cast on 51 sts. Work 1 left cable pat, 1 fan pat and 1 right cable pat, [rep Rows 1–20] 19 times. Place remaining 51 sts on a st holder or length of yarn.

Finishing

Block panels to size. Sew strips tog, alternating panels, beg and ending with Panel A.

Knit Tip: As afghan does not have an added border on sides, save a Panel A with no yarn joins on LH edge and another with no joins on RH edge for left and right edges.

Top Border

Sl 269 sts from holders onto a circular needle.

Work in garter st for 2 inches, ending with a WS row.

Row 1 (RS): K2, *ssk, rep from * to last st, k1.

Row 2: K2, *yo, k1, rep from * to last st, k1.

Row 3: Knit across.

Bind off all sts knitwise. ◆

Quick Lacy Throw

Design by Carol May

Worked with three strands held together throughout, this cozy afghan is the perfect project for a snowbound weekend.

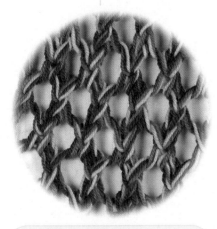

Skill Level
Beginner*

Finished Size
Approximately 42 x 56 inches

Materials
- Plymouth Encore worsted weight 75 percent acrylic/25 percent wool yarn (200 yds/100g per ball): 4 balls each light green #801, medium green #9401, dark green #1604
- Size 15 (10mm) 29-inch circular needle or size needed to obtain gauge
- Tapestry needle
- 9-inch-wide piece of stiff cardboard

Gauge
6 sts = 4 inches/10cm in garter st

To save time, take time to check gauge.

Pattern Notes
Throw is worked with 1 strand of each color held tog throughout.

Circular needle is used to accomodate large number of sts. Do not join at end of row.

Afghan
Using 3 strands of yarn, loosely cast on 69 sts. Knit every row until there are 3 ridges of garter st, ending with a WS row.

Row 1 (RS): K3, *k2tog, yo, rep from * to last 4 sts, end k4.

Row 2: Knit across.

Row 3: K4, *yo, k2tog, rep from * to last 3 sts, end k3.

Row 4: Knit across.

Rep Rows 1–4 until piece measures 54 inches or 2 inches less than desired length.

Work in garter st until there are 3 ridges on front of work. Bind off all sts loosely and knitwise.

Tassels
Make 4

Using 3 strands tog, wrap 24 times around stiff cardboard. Cut yarn, leaving a 12-inch end. Thread strands into tapestry needle, run strands around all strands at 1 end of cardboard several times, pulling tight. Fasten off securely. Cut all strands at opposite end. With separate length of yarn, wrap tassel tightly about 2 inches below top, fasten off and run ends into tassel. Trim bottom, then fasten to corner of throw with ends at top. ◆

Reversible Square-in-a-Square

Design by Annette McRell

Inspired by a classic American quilt design, this reversible afghan can go anywhere, fitting any style of home decorations.

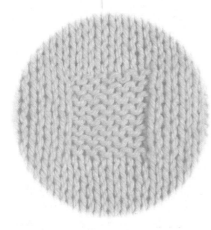

Skill Level
Beginner*

Finished Size
Approximately 40 x 50 (50 x 60) inches

Instructions are given for smaller size, with larger size in parentheses. When only 1 number is given, it applies to both sizes.

Materials
- Plymouth Encore Chunky bulky weight 75 percent acrylic/25 percent wool yarn (143 yds/100g per ball): 8(11) balls Aran #256
- Size 9 (5.5mm) needles
- Size 10 (6mm) needles or size needed to obtain gauge
- Tapestry needle

Gauge
14 sts = 4 inches/10cm in St st with larger needles

To save time, take time to check gauge.

Afghan
With smaller needles, cast on 134(162) sts. Knit 6 rows. Change to larger needles and beg pat.

Row 1: K4, *k14, p14, rep from * to last 18 sts, k14, k4.

Row 2: K4, *p14, k14, rep from * to last 18 sts, p14, k4.

Rows 3–6: [Rep Rows 1 and 2] twice.

Row 7: K4, *k4, p6, k4, p4, k6, p4, rep from * to last 18 sts, k4, p6, k4, k4.

Row 8: K4, *p4, k6, p4, k4, p6, k4, rep from * to last 18 sts, p4, k6, p4, k4.

Rows 9–14: [Rep Rows 7 and 8] 3 times.

Rows 15–20: [Rep Rows 1 and 2] 3 times.

Row 21: K4, *p14, k14, rep from * to last 18 sts, p14, k4.

Row 22: K4, *k14, p14, rep from * to last 18 sts, k14, k4.

Rows 23–26: [Rep Rows 21 and 22] twice.

Row 27: K4, *p4, k6, p4, k4, p6, k4, rep from * to last 18 sts, p4, k6, p4, k4.

Row 28: K4, *k4, p6, k4, p4, k6, p4, rep from * to last 18 sts, k4, p6, k4, k4.

Rows 29–34: [Rep Rows 27 and 28] 3 times.

Row 35–40: [Rep Rows 21 and 22] 3 times.

Rep Rows 1–40 for pat.

Rep Rows 1–40 until piece measures approximately 48(58) inches, ending with Row 19 or 39.

Knit 6 rows. Bind off all sts. ◆

Sand Dunes Afghan

Design by Laura Polley

The thick, warm fabric of this afghan makes it great for the den or cabin. The easy overall cable pattern gives the impression of complexity.

Skill Level
Intermediate***

Finished Size
Approximately 54 x 67½ inches

Materials
- Plymouth Encore Chunky bulky weight 75 percent acrylic/25 percent wool yarn (143 yds/100g per ball): 34 balls off-white #256
- Size 15 (10mm) 32-inch circular needle or size needed to obtain gauge
- Cable needle
- Tapestry needle

Gauge
15 sts and 15 rows = 4 inches/10cm in pat with 2 strands held tog

To save time, take time to check gauge.

Pattern Notes
Afghan is worked with 2 strands of yarn held tog throughout.

Circular needle is used to accomodate large number of sts. Do not join at end of row.

Special Abbreviations
BC (Back Cross): Sl next 3 sts to cn and hold in back, k3, k3 from cn.

FC (Front Cross): Sl next 3 sts to cn and hold in front, k3, k3 from cn.

Pattern Stitch
Sand Dunes Pat (multiple of 12 sts + 2)

Rows 1 and 5 (RS): Knit across.

Rows 2, 4 and 6: Purl across.

Row 3: K1, *FC, k6, rep from * to last st, end k1.

Row 7: K1, *k6, BC, rep from * to last st, end k1.

Row 8: Purl across.

Rep Rows 1–8 for pat.

Afghan
With 2 strands of yarn, cast on 194 sts.

Rows 1–240: [Work Rows 1–8 of pat] 30 times. Piece should measure approximately 64 inches from beg.

Bind off all sts, leaving last st on RH needle.

Finishing
***Note:** Pick up and k sts along edge at a rate of 2 sts for every 3 sts or rows on all 4 edges. This will give the number of sts given for each border section.*

Left Border
Turn afghan ¼-turn clockwise so left edge is at top. Counting loop on RH needle as first st, pick up and k 160 more sts along afghan edge. (161 sts)

Turn and work border in rows.

Row 1 (WS): P1, *k1, p1 rep from * across.

Row 2: K2, *p1, k1, rep from * to last st, k1.

Row 3: P2, *k1, p1, rep from * to last st, p1.

Row 4: K1, *p1, k1, rep from * across.

Rows 5–7: Rep Rows 1–3.

Bind off in pat as Row 4, leaving last st on needle.

Bottom Border
Turn afghan clockwise again, so bottom (cast-on) edge is at top. Counting loop on RH needle as first st, pick up and k 5 sts along edge of left border and 129 more sts along afghan edge. (135 sts)

Work as for left border, leaving last st on needle.

Right Border
Turn afghan clockwise again, so right edge is at top. Counting loop on RH needle as first st, pick up and k 5 sts along edge of bottom border and 161 more sts along afghan edge. (167 sts)

Work as for left border, leaving last st on needle.

Top Border
Turn afghan clockwise again, so bound off edge is at top. Counting loop on RH needle as first st, pick up and k 5 sts along edge of right border, 129 sts across bound off edge, then 6 more sts along side edge of left border. (141 sts) ◆

Jiffy Rib Afghan

Design by Barbara Venishnick

The surprise element of this design is the I-cord fringe. It is knitted on to look like a continuation of the knitted ribs.

Skill Level
Easy**

Finished Size
Approximately 40 x 48 inches (excluding fringe)

Materials
- Cleckheaton Mohair 12 ply bulky weight 92 percent mohair/4 percent wool/4 percent nylon yarn (110 yds/50g per ball) from Plymouth Yarn: 10 balls light blue #252
- Plymouth Wildflower DK weitht 51 percent cotton/49 percent acrylic yarn (137 yds/50g per ball): 9 balls light blue #33
- Size 10 (6mm) double-pointed and 40-inch circular needles or size needed to obtain gauge
- Tapestry needle

Gauge
13 sts and 18 rows = 4 inches/10cm in pat with 1 strand of each yarn held tog

To save time, take time to check gauge.

Pattern Notes
Afghan is worked with 1 strand of each color held tog throughout.

Circular needle is used to accomodate large number of sts. Do not join at end of row.

Reserve 1 ball of mohair and an equal amount of cotton for fringe.

Afghan
With 1 strand of each yarn, cast on 129 sts.

Row 1 (RS): K1 tbl, *k2, p3, rep from * to last 3 sts, end k2, wyif, sl last st purlwise.

Row 2: K1 tbl, purl to last st, sl 1 purlwise.

Rep Rows 1 and 2 for pat until piece measures 48 inches, ending with Row 2.

Bind off all sts in pat.

I-Cord Fringe
With dpn and 1 strand of each yarn, pick up and k 1 st in each of 2 k sts of first rib. Cast on 2 more sts (a total of 4 sts). Do not turn.

*Sl all sts to other end of needle, bring yarn across back of work, k4. Do not turn. Rep from * until a total of 13 rows of I-Cord have been worked.

Cut yarn and draw through all sts using a tapestry needle. Weave ends into cord.

Work an I-Cord fringe at top and bottom of each knit rib. ◆

Autumn Aran Afghan

Design by Diane Zangl

Easy stitches, big needles and three strands of yarn combine in this autumn-hued afghan.

Skill Level
Easy**

Finished Size
Approximately 45 x 52 inches (blocked)

Materials
- Plymouth Encore worsted weight 75 percent acrylic/25 percent wool yarn (200 yds/100g per ball): 11 balls natural #256 (MC)
- Plymouth Encore Colorspun worsted weight 75 percent acrylic/25 percent wool yarn (200 yds/100g per ball): 3 balls caramel tweed #7172 (CC)
- Size 15 (10mm) needles or size needed to obtain gauge
- Cable needle
- Tapestry needle

Gauge
9 sts and 12 rows = 4 inches/10cm in St st with 3 strands of yarn

To save time, take time to check gauge.

Pattern Notes
For color A, hold 3 strands of MC tog. For color B, hold 2 strands of MC and 1 strand of CC tog.

To avoid holes when changing colors, always pick up new color from under old.

Special Abbreviation
C6 (Cable 6): Sl 3 sts to cn and hold in front, k3, k3 from cn.

Right Panel Pat
Row 1 (RS): With B, sl 1, k15, with A, k3, p1, k6, p1, k3.

Row 2 and remaining WS rows: With A, p3, k1, p6, k1, p3, with B, p12, k4.

Row 3: With B, sl 1, k15, with A, k3, pl, C6, p1, k3.

Rows 5, 7, 9, and 11: Rep Row 1.

Row 12: Rep Row 2.

Rep Rows 1–12 for pat.

Beg pat
With B, cast on 30 sts. Sl first st of every RS row, knit 5 rows.

[Work Rows 1–12] 13 times, rep Rows 1–4.

Cut A, and with B only, knit 6 rows. Bind off all sts.

Left Panel Pat
Row 1 (RS): With A, k3, p1, k6, p1, k3, with B, k16.

Row 2 and remaining WS rows: With B, sl 1, k3, p12, with A, p3, k1, p6, k1, p3.

Row 3: With A, k3, p1, C6, p1, k3, with B, k16.

Rows 5, 7, 9 and 11: Rep Row 1.

Row 12: Rep Row 2.

Rep Rows 1–12 for pat.

Beg pat
With B, cast on 30 sts. Sl first st of every WS row, knit 5 rows.

[Work Rows 1–12] 13 times, rep Rows 1–4.

Cut color A, and with color B only, knit 6 rows. Bind off all sts.

Center Panel Pat
Row 1 (RS): With B, k15, with A, k3, p1, k6, p1, k3, with B, k15.

Row 2 and remaining WS rows: With B, p15, with A, p3, k1, p6, k1, p3, with B, p15.

Row 3: With B, k15, with A, k3, p1, C6, p1, k3, with B, k15.

Rows 5, 7, 9 and 11: Rep Row 1.

Row 12: Rep Row 2.

Rep Rows 1–12 for pat.

Beg pat
With B, cast on 44 sts. Knit 5 rows.

[Work Rows 1–12] 13 times, rep Rows 1–4.

Cut color A, and with color B only, knit 6 rows. Bind off all sts.

Finishing
Sew panels tog. Block. ◆

Cabin in the Woods

*W*hat better place to cuddle with your honey than in a cozy cabin or lodge. Whether you're relaxing on the porch after a day hiking in the woods or spending a cool evening sitting around a campfire, you'll enjoy snuggling in a soft, warm afghan.

Chapter 8

Greek Key Afghan

Design by Linda W. Cyr

The easy-to-follow pattern stitch is comprised of knit and purls with a double row of contrasting single crochet to give a firm finished edge.

Skill Level
Easy**

Finished Size
Approximately 46 x 54 inches

Materials
- Plymouth Encore worsted weight 75 percent acrylic/25 percent wool yarn (200 yds/100g per ball): 8 balls medium blue #436 (MC), 2 balls black #217 (CC)
- Size 8 (5mm) 24-inch circular needle or size needed to obtain gauge
- Size K/10½ (6.5mm) crochet hook
- Tapestry needle

Gauge
21 sts and 18 rows = 4 inches/10cm in patt

To save time, take time to check gauge.

Afghan
With MC, cast on 246 sts. Work 4 rows garter st.

Keeping first and last 2 sts in garter st for selvage throughout, work pat from chart, beg with Row 1, rep [Rows 1–20] 12 times.

Work 4 rows garter st. Bind off all sts.

Finishing
Block afghan to finished measurements.

With 2 strands of CC, work 2 rnds of sc around edge of afghan, working 3 sc in each corner. ◆

STITCH KEY
☐ K on RS, p on WS
⊟ P on RS, k on WS

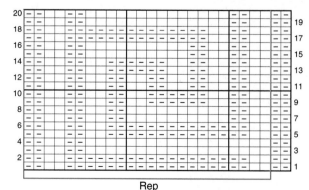

Rep

GREEK KEY AFGHAN

Ragg & Riches Afghan

Design by Laura Polley

This handsome afghan features mitered rib borders, and an easy knit-purl central pattern with the look of ragg yarn.

Skill Level

Intermediate***

Finished Size

Approximately 54 x 68 inches

Materials

- Plymouth Encore worsted weight 75 percent acrylic/25 percent wool yarn (200 yds/100g per ball): 11 balls grey #194 (A), 8 balls white #208 (B), 2 balls charcoal #520 (C)
- Size 11 (8mm) 32-inch circular needle
- Size 13 (9mm) 32-inch or longer circular needle or size needed to obtain gauge
- Tapestry needle
- 5½-inch-wide piece of cardboard

Gauge

12¼ sts and 18½ rows = 4 inches/10cm in Chart B pat with larger needles and 2 strands of yarn

To save time, take time to check gauge.

Pattern Notes

Afghan is worked with 2 strands of yarn held tog throughout.

Circular needle is used to accomodate large number of sts. Do not join at end of row.

Special Abbreviations

T2R (Twist 2 Right): K1 in front of 2nd st on LH needle leaving st on

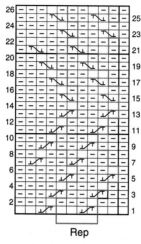

Rep

CHART A

Rep

CHART B

STITCH KEY

☐ K on RS, p on WS
⊟ P on RS, k on WS
⤢ T2R
⤡ T2L

needle, k1 in front of first st, sl both sts off needle at once.

T2L (Twist 2 Left): K1 in back of 2nd st on LH needle leaving st on needle, k1 in front of first st, sl both sts off needle at once.

M1K (Make 1 Knit): With yarn on WS, pick up running thread between sts and place on LH needle, k1 in back loop.

M1P (Make 1 Purl): With yarn on RS, pick up running thread between sts and

place on LH needle, p1 in back loop.

Afghan

With smaller needle and 2 strands of C held tog, cast on 147 sts. Knit 2 rows.

Change to larger needle and 2 strands of A, work pat Rows 1–26 from Chart A.

Change to smaller needle and 2 strands of C, knit 2 rows.

Change to larger needle, using 1 strand of A and 1 strand of B held tog, work Rows 1–15 from Chart B, then rep Rows 2–15 until piece measures approximately 54 inches from beg, ending with Row 14.

Change to smaller needle and 2 strands of C, knit 2 rows.

Change to larger needle and 2 strands of A, work pat Rows 1–26 from Chart A. Piece should measure approximately 59¾ inches from beg.

Change to smaller needle and 2 strands of C, knit 2 rows. Bind off all sts.

Finishing

Note: When working inc at each end of RS rows, use M1K or M1P as needed to maintain established rib pat.

Side borders

With smaller needle and 2 strands of C, pick up and k 190 sts along side (long) edge of afghan. Knit 1 row.

Inc row (RS): Using 1 strand of A and 1 strand of B, k1, *M1K, k4, rep from * to last st, M1K, k1. (238 sts)

Next row: P2 (selvage sts), *k2, p2, rep from * to last 2 sts, p2 (selvage sts).

Next row: K2, M1K, *p2, k2, rep from * to last 2 sts, M1K, k2. (240 sts)

Continue in established rib pat, inc 1 st in pat inside selvages at each end every RS row until there are 246 sts, ending with a WS row. Bind off all sts in pat. Rep for other side.

End borders

With smaller needle and 1 strand of A and 1 strand of B, pick up and k 147 sts across end of afghan. Do not pick up sts in edges of side borders.

Inc row (WS): P2 (selvage sts), k2, p1, *M1P, k2, p1, rep from * to last 4 sts, M1P, k2, p2 (selvage sts). (194 sts)

Work in established rib pat, inc as for side borders until there are 202 sts, ending with a WS row. Bind off all sts in pat. Rep for other end.

Sew border corners tog.

Tassels

Make 4

Cut 18-inch piece of C and lay aside.
Wrap C around cardboard 25 times.

Cut strands at 1 end, fold in half, wrap 18-inch length around center of cut strands several times and tie securely. Working about 1 inch below top of tassel, wrap several times around entire tassel, fasten off, then thread end back to top of tassel and use it to tie tassel to corner of afghan. Trim ends if needed. ◆

Striped Forest Afghan

Design by Nazanin S. Fard

This is a beautiful afghan using two different cable patterns in strips of two shades of green, joined using a variegated yarn and reverse crochet stitching.

Skill Level
Intermediate***

Finished Size
Approximately 62 x 70 inches

Materials
- Plymouth Encore worsted weight 75 percent acrylic/25 percent wool yarn (200 yds/100g per ball): 8 balls dark green #1233 (A), 9 balls light green #1231 (B)
- Plymouth Encore Colorspun worsted weight 75 percent acrylic/25 percent wool yarn (200 yds/100g per ball): 4 balls variegated #7172
- Size 8 (5mm) needles or size needed to obtain gauge
- Cable needle
- Size G/6 (4mm) crochet hook
- Tapestry needle

Gauge
16 sts and 30 rows = 4 inches/ 10cm in St st

To save time, take time to check gauge.

Special Abbreviations
FC (Front Cross): Sl 2 sts to cn and hold in front, p1, k2 from cn.

BC (Back Cross): Sl 1 st to cn and hold in back, k2, p1 from cn.

Panel 1
Make 10 with A

Cast on 16 sts. Work 3 ridges of garter st.

Row 1 and remaining WS rows: K4, p8, k4.

Row 2: K2, p2, sl next 2 sts to cn and hold in back, k2, k2 from cn, sl next 2 sts to cn and hold in front, k2, k2 from cn, p2, k2.

Row 4: K2, p2, k8, p2, k2.

Row 6: K2, p2, sl next 2 sts to cn and hold in front, k2, k2 from cn, sl next 2 sts to cn and hold in back, k2, k2 from cn, p2, k2.

Row 8: K2, p2, k8, p2, k2.

Rep Rows 1–8 for pat, end with 3 ridges of garter st (strip should measure 69 inches).

Panel 2
Make 9 with B

Cast on 19 sts. Work 3 ridges of garter st.

Row 1 (WS): K6, p4, k2, p2, k5.

Row 2: K2, p3, FC, BC, FC, p3, k2.

Row 3 and remaining WS rows: K2, k the knit sts and p the purl sts, end k2.

Row 4: K2, p4, sl next 2 sts to cn and hold in back, k2, k2 from cn, p2, k2, p3, k2. (19 sts)

Row 6: K2, p3, BC, FC, BC, p3, k2.

Row 8: K2, p3, k2, p2, sl next 2 sts to cn and hold in front, k2, k2 from cn, p4, k2.

Rep Rows 1–8 for pat, end with 3 ridges of garter st (strip should measure 69 inches).

Finishing
With crochet hook and CC, join panels as follows, beg with Panel 1 and alternating panels:

Row 1: Join yarn with sl st in first st, sc in every st on both panels (one panel 1, and one panel 2).

Row 2: Reverse sc in every sc to end. Fasten off.

Rep Rows 1 and 2 for all panels.

Work Rows 1 and 2 around outer edge of afghan. Fasten off.

Block afghan. ◆

Acorn Afghan

Design by Fatema Habibur-Rahman

This warm and cozy afghan is worked with two strands throughout. It's a fast and interesting project, even for a beginner.

Skill Level
Easy**

Finished Size
Approximately 50 x 55 inches

Materials
- Plymouth Encore worsted weight 75 percent acrylic/25 percent wool yarn (200 yds/100g per ball): 12 balls cranberry #560
- Size 15 (10mm) 29- or 36-inch circular needle or size needed to obtain gauge
- Tapestry needle

Gauge
6 sts = 4 inches/10cm in St st with 2 strands of yarn

To save time, take time to check gauge.

Pattern Notes
Circular needle is used to accomodate large number of sts. Do not join at end of row.

Afghan is worked with 2 strands of yarn held tog throughout.

Pattern Stitch
Acorn Stitch (multiple of 6 sts + 2)

Row 1 (WS): K1, *p5tog, [k1, p1, k1, p1, k1] into next st, rep from * to last st, k1.

Row 2: Purl across.

Row 3: K1, *[k1, p1, k1, p1, k1] into next st, p5tog, rep from * to last st, k1.

Row 4: Purl across.

Row 5: Knit, wrapping yarn around needle 3 times for each st.

Row 6: Purl, dropping extra loops.

Rep Rows 1–6 for pat.

Afghan
With 2 strands of yarn held tog, cast on 182 sts.

Work Rows 1–6 of pat until piece measures approximately 49 inches from beg, ending with Row 4. Bind off all sts loosely.

Finishing
Wet-block afghan. ◆

Alpaca Lap Robe

Design by Edie Eckman

Combine this lovely textured pattern with a soft alpaca yarn and you'll stay warm and cozy!

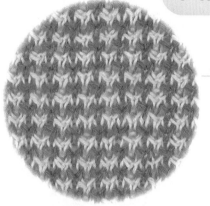

Skill Level
Intermediate***

Finished Size
Approximately 36 x 48 inches

Materials
- Indiecita worsted weight 100 percent alpaca yarn (102 yds/50g per ball) from Plymouth Yarn: 8 balls brown #208 (A), 3 balls off-white #100 (B)
- Size 8 (5mm) 29- or 36-inch circular needles
- Size 10 (6mm) needles or size needed to obtain gauge
- Tapestry needle

Gauge
11 sts and 28 rows = 4 inches/ 10 cm in pat

Gauge is not crucial in this project.

Pattern Notes
This is a loose-textured fabric and is difficult to measure. Gauges are approximate. If your finished pieces are significantly different in size, you may need to adjust number of sts picked up for borders. Borders are worked back and forth on circular needles.

Special Abbreviations
K1b: Knit in row below

Pattern Stitch
Row 1 (RS): With B, k1, *k1b, k1, rep from *.

Row 2: With B, knit.

Row 3: With A, k2, k1b, *k1, k1b, rep from * to last 2 sts, k2.

Row 4: With A, knit.

Rep Rows 1–4 for pat.

Afghan Strip
Make 3

With larger needles and A, cast on 31 sts loosely. Knit 1 row.

Beg pat st and work even until piece measures 11 inches. Piece should be approximately square at this point.

With A only, work even in pat until piece measures 22 inches from beg.

Using both colors, work even in pat until piece measures 33 inches from beg.

With A only, work even in pat until piece measures 44 inches from beg, ending with a WS row. Bind off loosely in pat.

Finishing
Block strips. Referring to photo, sew strips tog in a checkerboard pat.

Borders
*With smaller needles and A, RS facing, pick up and k 176 sts from 1 long edge of afghan. Knit 3 rows (2 garter st ridges). With B, knit 2 rows. With A, knit 4 rows. Bind off all sts. Rep from * for remaining long edge.

*With A, pick up and k 140 sts along short ends of borders just worked and short edge of afghan. Work border pat as for long edges. Rep from * for remaining edge. ◆

Sonoran Pathways

Design by Kathleen Brklacich Sasser

Worked with two stands of yarn throughout, this afghan features an impressive central geometric design and complementary border.

Skill Level
Intermediate***

Finished Size
Approximately 49½ x 61½ inches

Material
- Plymouth Galway worsted weight 100 percent wool yarn (230 yds/100g per ball): 10 balls Aran #01 (MC), 6 balls gold #60 (A), 8 balls dark gold #95 (B)
- Size 10 (6mm) 36-inch circular needle or size needed to obtain gauge
- Tapestry needle

Gauge
13 sts and 18 rows = 4 inches/ 10cm in St st and color pat with 2 strands of yarn

To save time, take time to check gauge.

Pattern Notes
Afghan is worked using 2 strands of yarn held tog throughout.

Wind a separate ball or butterfly of yarn for each color section.

To avoid holes at color changes, pick up new color under old.

Afghan
With 2 strands of B, cast on 164 sts.

Referring to chart, and beg with a WS row, knit 7 rows, then beg pat, keeping 5 selvage sts at each edge in garter st throughout and working center 154 sts in color pat and St st.

When color pat is completed, work last 7 rows in B and garter st. Bind off all sts after completing Row 280 of chart. ◆

**SONORAN PATHWAYS
UPPER LEFT**

COLOR KEY
- ☐ Aran (MC)
- ▨ Gold (A)
- ▩ Dark gold (B)

SONORAN PATHWAYS
UPPER RIGHT

**SONORAN PATHWAYS
LOWER LEFT**

COLOR KEY
☐ Aran (MC)
▨ Gold (A)
▧ Dark gold (B)

138
130
120
110
100
90
80
70
60
50
40
30
20
10
2

**SONORAN PATHWAYS
LOWER RIGHT**

American West Afghan

Design by Jean Schafer-Albers

Savor the flavor of the West when you knit his lovely afghan with its vibrant colors.

Skill Level
Advanced****

Finished Size
Approximately 39 x 51 inches

Materials
- Plymouth Encore worsted weight 75 percent acrylic/25 percent wool yarn (200 yds/100g per ball): 2 balls bright royal #133 (A), 1 ball double chocolate #599 (B), 2 balls cream #256 (C), 4 balls burnt sienna #999 (D), 2 balls orange #1383 (E), 3 balls medium forest #1233 (F), 1 ball butternut #1014 (G)
- Size 10 (8mm) 36-inch or longer circular needle or size needed to obtain gauge
- Tapestry needle

Gauge
14 sts and 20 rows = 4 inches/ 10cm in St st

To save time, take time to check gauge.

Pattern Notes
Circular needle is used to accomodate large number of sts. Do not join at end of row.

Afghan is worked in St st with 2 strands of yarn held tog throughout.

Afghan
With 2 strands of A, cast on 133 sts.

Rows 1–7: Beg with a WS row, work in St st for hem.

Row 8 (RS): Purl across. (turning ridge)

Rows 9–14: Work 6 rows with A.

Rows 15–30: Work 16 rows with B.

Rows 31–33: Work 3 rows with C.

Row 34 (RS): Work Row 1 of Chart A and *at the same time,* inc 21 sts evenly across row. (154 sts)

Rows 35–47: Complete Chart A pat.

Row 48 (RS): Work with A, *at the same time,* dec 21 sts evenly across row. (133 sts)

Rows 49 and 50: Work 2 more rows with A.

Rows 51–66: Work 16 rows with F.

Rows 67–86: Rep Rows 31–50.

Rows 87–95: Work 9 rows with B.

Rows 96–100: Work 5 rows with C.

Rows 101–114: Work 14 rows with F.

Rows 115–117: Work 3 rows with A.

Rows 118–133: Work 16 rows with D.

Rows 134–162: Beg with a RS row, work Chart B from right to left over first 67 sts, then work from left to right over remaining 66 sts, reversing image and working center st only once.

Rows 163–178: Work 16 rows with D.

Rows 179–181: Work 3 rows with A.

Rows 182–195: Work 14 rows with F.

Rows 196–200: Work 5 rows with C.

Rows 201–208: Work 8 rows with B.

Rows 209–211: Work 3 rows with A.

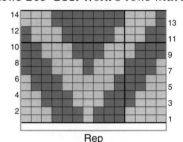

Rep

CHART A

COLOR KEY

- Burnt sienna (D)
- Orange (E)
- Butternut (G)

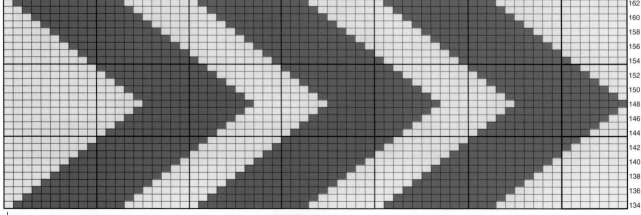

CHART B

center

Rows 212–225: Rep Rows 34–47. (154 sts)

Row 226 (RS): Work with C, *at the same time,* dec 21 sts evenly across row. (133 sts)

Rows 227 and 228: Work 2 more rows with C.

Rows 229–244: Work 16 rows with F.

Rows 245–250: Work 6 rows with A.

Row 251 (WS): Knit 1 row for turning ridge.

Rows 252–258: Knit 7 rows in St st with A for hem. Bind off all sts.

Finishing

Turn hems on turning ridge and sew in place.

Work side edges as follows:

With RS facing, using A, pick up and k 1 st for every st along side edges. On next row, bind off purlwise. ◆

Embossed Diamonds Afghan

Design by Barbara Venishnick

Everything about this afghan is oversized. The stitch is a large raised diamond arranged in long chains and ending in flamboyant tassels. It's fun to knit!

Skill Level
Intermediate***

Finished Size
Approximately 51 x 60 inches

Materials
- Plymouth Encore worsted weight 75 percent acrylic/25 percent wool yarn (200 yds/100g per ball): 10 balls beige #240 (A), 4 balls brown #1444 (B)
- Size 10 (6mm) needles or size needed to obtain gauge
- 33 bobbins
- Size H/8 (5mm) crochet hook
- Tapestry needle

Gauge
16 sts and 21⅓ rows = 4 inches/10cm in pat

To save time, take time to check gauge.

Pattern Notes
Work in intarsia technique, using a separate bobbin or butterfly of yarn for each vertical color section.

When changing colors, pick up new color under old to avoid holes.

Special Abbreviations
M1 (Make 1): Inc by purling into row below in adjacent st of same color. All inc and dec are made on WS rows.

P2togb (P2tog through back loop): Insert RH needle through back of next 2 purl sts from left to right, p2tog in this position.

Selvage st (S): Knit first st of every row tbl, work to within 1 st of end, sl last st of every row purlwise wyif. Both selvage sts are worked in color A.

Pattern Stitch
Embossed Diamond Patt (multiple of 26 sts + 1 + 2 selvage sts)

Row 1 (RS): S, k1A, [p3B, k19A, p3B, k1A] 8 times, S.

Row 2: S, p1A, [M1A, k3B, p2togA, p15A, p2togbA, k3B, M1A, p1A] 8 times, S.

Row 3: S, k2A, [p3B, k17A, p3B, k3A] 8 times, end last rep k2A, S.

Row 4: S, p2A, [M1A, k3B, p2togA, p13A, p2togbA, k3B, M1A, p3A] 8 times, end last rep p2A, S.

Row 5: S, k3A, [p3B, k15A, p3B, k5A] 8 times, end last rep k3A, S.

Row 6: S, p3A, [M1A, k3B, p2togA, p11A, p2togbA, k3B, M1A, p5A] 8 times, end last rep p3A, S.

Row 7: S, k4A, [p3B, k13A, p3B, k7A] 8 times, end last rep k4A, S.

Row 8: S, p4A, [M1A, k3B, p2togA, p9A, p2togbA, k3B, M1A, p7A] 8 times, end last rep p4A, S.

Row 9: S, k5A, [p3B, k11A, p3B, k9A] 8 times, end last rep k5A, S.

Row 10: S, p5A, [M1A, k3B, p2togA, p7A, p2togbA, k3B, M1A, p9A] 8 times, end last rep p5A, S.

Row 11: S, k6A, [p3B, k9A, p3B, k11A] 8 times, end last rep k6A, S.

Row 12: S, p6A, [M1A, k3B, p2togA, p5A, p2togbA, k3B, M1A, p11A] 8 times, end last rep p6A, S.

Row 13: S, k7A, [p3B, k7A, p3B, k13A] 8 times, end last rep k7A, S.

Row 14: S, p7A, [M1A, k3B, p2togA, p3A, p2togbA, k3B, M1A, p13A] 8 times, end last rep p7A, S.

Row 15: S, k8A, [p3B, k5A, p3B, k15A] 8 times, end last rep k8A, S.

Row 16: S, p8A, [M1A, k3B, p2togA, p1A, p2togbA, k3B, M1A, p15A] 8 times, end last rep p8A, S.

Row 17: S, k9A, [p3B, k3A, p3B, k17A] 8 times, end last rep k9A, S.

Row 18: S, p9A, [M1A, k3B, p3togA, k3B, M1A, p17A] 8 times, end last rep p9A, S.

Row 19: S, k10A, [p3B, k1A, p3B, k19A] 8 times, end last rep k10A, S.

Row 20: S, p8A, [p2togbA, k3B, M1A, p1A, M1A, k3B, p2togA, p15A] 8 times, end last rep p8A, S.

Row 21: S, k9A, [p3B, k3A, p3B, k17A] 8 times, end last rep k9A, S.

Row 22: S, p7A, [p2togbA, k3B, M1A, p3A, M1A, k3B, p2togA, p13A] 8 times, end last rep p7A, S.

Row 23: S, k8A, [p3B, k5A, p3B, k15A] 8 times, end last rep k8A, S.

Row 24: S, p6A, [p2togbA, k3B, M1A, p5A, M1A, k3B, p2togA, p11A] 8 times, end last rep p6A, S.

Row 25: S, k7A, [p3B, k7A, p3B, k13A] 8 times, end last rep k7A, S.

Row 26: S, p5A, [p2togbA, k3B, M1A, p7A, M1A, k3B, p2togA, p9A] 8 times, end last rep p5A, S.

Row 27: S, k6A, [p3B, k9A, p3B, k11A] 8 times, end last rep k6A, S.

Row 28: S, p4A, [p2togbA, k3B, M1A, p9A, M1A, k3B, p2togA, p7A] 8 times, end last rep p4A, S.

Row 29: S, k5A, [p3B, k11A, p3B, k9A] 8 times, end last rep k5A, S.

Row 30: S, p3A, [p2togbA, k3B, M1A, p11A, M1A, k3B, p2togA, p5A] 8 times, end last rep p3A, S.

Row 31: S, k4A, [p3B, k13A, p3B, k7A] 8 times, end last rep k4A, S.

Row 32: S, p2A, [p2togbA, k3B, M1A, p13A, M1A, k3B, p2togA, p3A] 8 times, end last rep p2A, S.

Row 33: S, k3A, [p3B, k15A, p3B, k5A] 8 times, end last rep k3A, S.

Row 34: S, p1A, [p2togbA, k3B, M1A, p15A, M1A, k3B, p2togA, p1A] 8 times, S.

Row 35: S, k2A, [p3B, k17A, p3B, k3A] 8 times, end last rep k2A, S.

Row 36: S, p2togbA, [k3B, M1A, p17A, M1A, k3B, p3togA] 8 times, end last rep p2togA, S.

Rep Rows 1–36 for pat.

Afghan

With A, cast on 211 sts. Work [Rows 1–36] 9 times.

With RS facing, bind off all sts with A.

Side Edging

With crochet hook and A, work 1 sc in each st along edge of afghan. Rep for other side.

Tassels
Make 18

With A, wrap yarn around a 6-inch-long ruler or piece of cardboard 20 times. With A, cut a length of yarn and tie top of tassel together tightly by inserting

yarn in center of ring formed around ruler. Cut bottom open. With B, wrap around tassel 1 inch down from top, 3 or 4 times. Tie tightly and poke ends inside tassel.

With yarn used to tie top of tassel, use a tapestry needle to sew one tassel to pointed end of each diamond all along top and bottom edges.

Press side edges lightly. Allow wide sections of diamonds at top and bottom edges to roll up. ◆

Special Thanks

We would like to thank Plymouth Yarn Company for providing all the yarn used in this book.
We also appreciate the help provided by Uyvonne Bigham and the Plymouth staff
throughout the publishing process. It's been great working with them.
We also thank the talented knitting designers whose work is featured in this collection.

Uyvonne Bigham
Rainbow Blocks Baby Afghan, 62
Warm & Cuddly Baby Afghan, 64
Kente Afghan for Kwaanza, 96
Christmas Ornaments Afghan, 108

Dixie Butler
Candy Cane Afghan, 94

Sue Childress
Butterfly Fantasy Baby Blanket, 66

Linda W. Cyr
Greek Key Afghan, 156

Edie Eckman
Dad's Drop-Stitch Throw, 42
Homespun Stripes, 136
Alpaca Lap Robe, 164

Joyce Englund
3-D Diamonds Afghan, 102
Cross-Stitch Squares, 138

Nazanin S. Fard
Counterpane Afghan, 28
Rainbow Baby Afghan, 68
Striped Forest Afghan, 160

Fatema Habibur-Rahman
Autumn Lace Lap Warmer, 44
Counterpane Log Afghan, 120
Acorn Afghan, 162

Lynnette Harter
Blue Christmas Afghan, 100

Shari Haux
Raspberry Afghan, 46
Eyelet Lace Afghan, 140

Jacqueline W. Hoyle
Country Garden Mosaic, 36
Wheelchair Throw, 57

Frances Hughes
Little Huggy Baby Blanket, 70
Candlelight Christmas Afghan, 92

Katharine Hunt
Inside Out Afghan, 128
Diagonal Squares Afghan, 130
Cable & Fans Afghan, 142

Kathleen Power Johnson
By the Sea, 20
Summer Garden Coverlet, 26
Lace & Lavender, 32

Bonnie Lively
Baby Animal Sampler, 84

Elizabeth Mattfield
Dover Road, 16
Trip-Round-the-World Afghan, 126

Carol May
Triangles on Point Afghan, 122
Quick Lacy Throw, 144

Sheryl McBreen
Climbing Roses, 34

Annette McRell
Reversible Square-in-a-Square
    Afghan, 146

Laura Polley
Little Buds Afghan, 14
Soft-as-a-Cloud Baby Afghan, 72
Cathedral Windows Afghan, 104
Raspberry Parfait Afghan, 116
Sand Dunes Afghan, 148
Ragg & Riches Afghan, 158

Kathleen Brklacich Sasser
Spencer the Elephant Baby, 74
Sonoran Pathways, 166

Jean Schafer-Albers
American West Afghan, 172

E. J. Slayton
Pine Forest Afghan, 106

Ann E. Smith
Diamonds Light & Lofty, 48
Easy Shells Baby Blanket, 78

JoAnne Turcotte
Christmas Forest Afghan, 98

Barbara Venishnick
Lazy Man's Plaid, 8
Ebb Tide, 18
Garden Path, 30
Northern Lights, 50
Tibetan Check Afghan, 124
Jiffy Rib Afghan, 150
Embossed Diamonds Afghan, 174

Jill Wolcott
Herringbone Pie Blanket, 54
Tilt-a-Whirl Baby Afghan, 82

Lois S. Young
Guy's Guernsey Afghan, 10
Lacy Twist Afghan, 12
Sumptuous Stripes Afghan, 52
Windowpane Afghan, 114

Diane Zangl
Blossoms & Buds, 24
Busy Blanket, 80
Patchwork Trio Afghan, 118
Autumn Aran Afghan, 152